One of the biggest issues procurement organizations face today is readying their leaders not only for the current environment but also for the ever-changing and exciting future of supply management. Today, unfortunately, we find many organizations having to search outside the function, as well as outside the company, when leadership positions become available. *The Global Procurement Leader's Handbook* is well positioned to change this by combining the experiential, practical, and systematic insights of a highly dynamic chief procurement officer, known for his transformational leadership, and a management consultant with decades of experience in coaching successful supply-management leaders and their employees. Rather than the typical theories and concepts, this handbook provides the necessary assessment tools to gauge your current leadership readiness and, more important, the tools for making improvements. It is positioned to become a standard for guiding the development of the next generation of supply-management leaders and reestablishing our own organizations as the suppliers of choice for the next CPO.

—Chris Sawchuk
Principal and Global Procurement Advisory Practice Leader
The Hackett Group

The Global Procurement Leader's Handbook stands apart from other books about procurement for three reasons. First, it is practical and easy to put to work quickly for improved results. Second, it provides you with frameworks that will help you and your organization enjoy consistent and sustainable improvement. Third, and most importantly, it is the first guide about procurement that I have ever seen that takes a comprehensive, strategic look at the subject, including: what it means to lead procurement with best practices; how to gain organizational commitment and engagement; how to be seen as a strategic leader in the organization and not merely as a support function; and specific ways to develop talent within the procurement function. If you want a guide to success and best practices in global procurement, this is a must-read book!

—Andrew Neitlich
Director, Center for Executive Coaching

The Global Procurement Leader's Handbook

The Global Procurement Leader's Handbook

Your Toolkit for Building and Maintaining a World-Class Procurement Function

Erik Stavrand and Chris Shanahan

Foreword by Willie Deese

SEAK LLC

THE GLOBAL PROCUREMENT LEADER'S HANDBOOK
Your Toolkit for Building and Maintaining a World-Class Procurement Function

Written by Erik Stavrand and Chris Shanahan

ISBN-13: 978-0996531603
ISBN-10: 0996531602

Editor: Bobbi Linkemer, www.WriteANonfictionBook.com
Book design: Peggy Nehmen, www.n-kcreative.com

SEAK LLC

Published by Seak, LLC
PO Box 511718
Punta Gorda, FL 33951-1718

www.GlobalProcurementLeadersHandbook.com

From Chris:

For my wife, Kate, and children, Grace, Ben, and Daniel,
for moving continents in supporting my career and
enabling me to contribute to this project.

From Erik:

This book is dedicated to my wife, Susan, whose support and unending
encouragement made the writing and rewriting of this book possible.

I also want to thank my editor, Bobbi Linkemer, and book designer, Peggy Nehmen.
They provided a steady hand and a ready knife for the jargon. They both pondered
retirement during (because of) this book, and I appreciate their perseverance.

Finally, thank you to my colleagues Patti Whitehouse, John Bolla, Markus Schaefer,
Jonathan O'Brien, and Iain Stewart. Each came forward with detailed, thoughtful
suggestions and I really appreciate their time and ideas.

Contents

Acknowledgments

✷ From Chris:

I have been very fortunate to work for a number of great companies and excellent leaders.

I would like to acknowledge Don Brockie, the financial controller at SmithKline Beecham in Dungarvan, Ireland, for his insistence that I complete my master's degree and David Malpiedi for hiring me at Becton Dickinson (BD) and trusting me in a leadership role in Europe, which has enabled me to share my experience in this book.

I would also like to thank Steve Sichak at BD for pushing me and creating additional opportunities for me.

Finally, I am grateful for the honor of leading a strong leadership team at BD. I would like to recognize Debra Utko, in particular, for her leadership in the sourcing process, as well as Stephanie Tighe, Roger Ambrose, Patrick Williams, Noelle Lee, Susan Gavigan, and Steve Livernois for their excellent management of the procurement function.

✷ From Erik:

This book is the result of more than twenty-five years of working with brilliant co-workers who were focused on doing high-quality work for demanding clients. This set of circumstances created an environment in which creativity is required, and collaboration is the rule. During my early consulting days, I was very fortunate to work for Bob Buckenmayer and Robin Cammish, who helped shape my strategic thinking and taught me about procurement. My co-workers during this period—Carlos Nicot, Iain Stewart, Jonathan O'Brien, Mark Hubbard, Richard Spoor, Philip Usherwood, Markus Schaefer, and Ron Guertin—embodied deep professional experience and a commitment to demonstrating the value of strategic procurement.

Demanding, smart clients push consultants to deliver new and meaningful value. Chris Shanahan, David Malpiedi, Debra Utko, John Bolla, Patti Whitehouse, Richard Spoor, and Willie Deese recognized and appreciated our efforts. I am forever grateful to them for their inspiration and support.

Foreword

The Global Procurement Leader's Handbook is a practical application manual that provides detailed, step-by-step frameworks and templates for building world-class procurement functions and achieving consistent and sustainable improvements. Together, Erik Stavrand and Chris Shanahan have more than fifty years of hands-on experience in procurement, which informs an insightful view of what is required of an organization, a leader, and a corporate environment to be successful.

The authors pose questions that require candid responses and present a structured methodology to drive predictable, repeatable outcomes. This handbook focuses on hard and soft methods for driving and leading change in complex environments; looks at the competence of the procurement leader, as well as the procurement organization; and assesses the readiness of the broader organization to embrace the challenge of becoming a world-class procurement function. Because the authors have worked in and with global companies, they bring a geographically diverse world-view, as well as a varied industry perspective.

The book leads off with a sweeping (and highly confidential) assessment of a company's readiness and willingness to do the difficult but necessary work required to become a world-class procurement organization. It questions whether the role of the procurement leader is positioned for success, which helps potential hires decide whether to accept a position if it is offered.

Once in the functional leadership role, the leader and his or her leadership team are responsible for developing a comprehensive plan for Procurement in support of the company's goals. The handbook then outlines a very thoughtful approach in three steps.

- **B-Building Blocks of Functional Leadership** presents the requisite tools and techniques required of every procurement leader.
- **U-Us: Our Relationships** explains how to clarify values, develop effective communications, build trust, and solicit the input of stakeholders.
- **Y-You: Your Leadership of the Function** addresses assessing competence and quality of work, designing new structures, aligning talent with future requirements, and establishing expectations.

There is a logical, detailed roadmap for what must be done coupled with understanding of what will work best within a particular organization. In my view, the quality of implementation almost always determines the outcome of any transformational activity. This book provides very helpful tips on what the leader must do, what the procurement organization must do, and what the broader organization must do to become a world-class procurement organization.

Over the last twenty-five years, I have had the opportunity to lead several successful procurement transformations in three different global companies within the pharmaceutical industry. I have also been the primary customer of a procurement transformation as the global head of Manufacturing and Supply Chain at one of those companies. I can say with certainty that, had this book existed twenty-five years ago, fifteen years ago, or even five years ago, it would have made my journeys much easier. There is no doubt in my mind that the successful outcomes I achieved would have been delivered faster and perhaps better if this handbook had been available.

The beauty of this handbook is that it takes into account all that is necessary to enable a successful procurement transformation—from procurement processes to organizational competence and readiness. From the hard to the soft skills (i.e., stakeholder engagement, formation and leadership of cross-functional teams, sourcing strategy) all are covered in the handbook in one convenient place.

Erik and Chris have hit the sweet spot with this handbook. It is instructional, educational, and dare I say inspirational because it is a personal account written by two people who *have been there, done that* many times with great success. If anyone tackling his or her first CPO assignment, or even a veteran of several procurement transformations, this book will become a frequently used and much-appreciated reference.

Willie A. Deese
Executive Vice President and President
Merck Manufacturing Division
Merck and Co. Inc.

Introduction

The Global Procurement Leader's Handbook is intended for practical application and covers the building blocks of procurement leadership. Before each topic are Topic Area Assessment Statements for your self-reflection. Review each statement from your perspective as a procurement leader. If you "fully agree" with each statement, you may not need to review the section and may choose to review another topic. If, however, you don't fully agree with one or more statements, we advise you to read that relevant section. In each topic, Erik explains the content and the context for application. Chris's view of the tool is from the perspective of the chief procurement officer (CPO) and includes frank assessments of what works and lessons he has learned along the way. Reference templates are provided for appropriate topics. *Note: The templates are also available online at www.globalprocurementleadershandbook.com.*

Once you are in the functional leadership role, it is time for you and your leadership team to develop a comprehensive plan for the procurement function. Our approach comprises three parts.

B–Building Blocks of Functional Leadership: the requisite tools and techniques that every procurement leader must demonstrate

- How will we create the future? *Determining the processes and tools for use across the function*
- Where will we focus our efforts? *Working with stakeholders to select the critical few areas to focus our resources and attention*
- How will we use our resources? *Developing consistent approaches to leading cross-functional teams*
- How will we ensure strategic thinking that links the needs of the business with the supply market of the future? *Applying proven approaches to generating business requirements, conducting strategic analysis, and developing stakeholder-relevant strategies*
- How will we assess and manage risk? *Separating the core causes of risk and managing them proactively*

U–Us: Our Relationships

- Who are we? *Clarifying our values and ensuring effective communications*
- How do we relate to others? *Building trusted relationships with others in alignment with their unique needs and perceptions*
- How do we listen to others? *Taking the pulse of the key constituents (stakeholders) and embracing their input*

Y–You: Your Leadership of the Function

- Can we *perform* as well as *lead*? *Assessing personal and organizational competence*
- Are we doing high-quality work? *Assessing the quality of the work performed*
- Are we structured appropriately? *Designing new structures to support and enable new capabilities in an efficient way*
- Do we have the right talent? *Ensuring that the talent priorities are aligned with future requirements*
- How high are our expectations? *Establishing your expectations of the procurement team and the organization*

This is not a book you are likely to read cover to cover; that is not its purpose. Rather, it is intended to provide value on a topical level. We recommend starting with the online assessment (nominal fee) on our website, www.globalprocurementleadershandbook.com. The results of this assessment will provide direction regarding topics worthy of additional review.

Contact us at erik@seakllc.com with questions.

1 100-Day Plan: Prioritizing Your Efforts to Ensure Success

Topic Area Assessment Statements

Review these statements from your perspective as a procurement leader. If you "strongly agree" with all of the statements, you may wish to skip to the next chapter. But, if you have some doubts about any of them, we recommend that you read this topic and engage in some self-reflection.

- I understand why I was selected for this role and what I must do first.
- I can rely on the management team to support me in my new role.
- I have a clear plan for how to organize and align my work with the highest-priority outcomes.
- I know how my efforts will be assessed and measured.
- I have the support infrastructure (HR, IT, Finance, etc.) in place to succeed.

Topic Introduction: 100-Day Plan Overview

Your time and attention are your most precious resources. Together, they signal to the organization where you will focus, how you analyze situations, and your direction and trajectory for the future. They will be the basis for all "first impressions." In short, you must have a clear plan on display, even if you are less organized behind the scenes!

Topic-Specific Nomenclature

As in many business entities, procurement professionals use a range of language with very specific definitions. The following terms and definitions are used in this section:

- ***Stakeholders*** – key constituents *inside* your company who are affected by the work of the procurement department or function
- ***Value proposition*** – the offerings procurement provides to customers in response to their needs
- ***Collaborative spend governance*** – the process of working with stakeholders to jointly agree on the priority categories/sub-categories for initial focus, the applicable sourcing approach, and the required team members and sponsor
- ***Support infrastructure*** – the functional support areas (IT, HR, Finance, Legal, etc.) required to implement change across the procurement function

Detailed Plan Development: Begins Before Day One

The creation of a comprehensive plan starts during the interview process. The following are some key questions to address before you take on the role:

- Are the right people interviewing you?
- Do they have a clear understanding of the prospective role?
- Are they honest about existing challenges?
- Do they have a vision for success?
- Do you think you can work with the hiring manager?
- How does your style complement the hiring manager's style?
- Do you have a compensation package that addresses your personal and family concerns so you can focus on the job?
- Are the required change-management supports and resources in place to achieve success?

Answers to each of these questions are important; their sum total will reflect whether or not this position is set up for success. Many organizations want the results (e.g., value, savings, risk management, innovation) from world-class procurement, but few understand the degree of change required or are ready to fully embark on the journey.

If the majority of the answers to the above questions are not favorable, *do not accept the position.* It is a true "no-win situation," and the only person who will succeed is your successor. Politely inform the recruitment team of the gaps between what they are seeking and what is possible. Offer to stay in touch. Don't be afraid to say *no* if *yes* will lead to inevitable failure.

The more common scenario, however, is a mixed result. Some of the questions lead to substandard answers, but the job is intriguing, so you deem it to be "worth the risk." Risk taking is the core of leadership. Go for it! With an objective view of the situation, you will have to shore up the weak areas.

Assuming you take the position as procurement leader, here are your key steps:

Before you do anything else, complete the Global Procurement Leader's Assessment at www.globalprocurementleadershandbook.com. It will help you identify the priority areas you need to address. Use these results and the following steps to develop a comprehensive 100-day plan.

Priority #1: Us—Our Relationships

Assess the stakeholders. Identify the "critical few," and book time to meet with them (in person, if at all possible; video or virtual meetings are the next best option).

Do the stakeholders

- Understand the value proposition of Procurement?
- Recognize the implications of their current behaviors with regard to the supply base?
- Know their role in spend governance?
- Appear approachable? (Can you build rapport with them?)
- Seem open to collaboration with peers (or do you sense competition)?
- Know the value you can bring?
- Understand the historical performance of the procurement function?
- Have challenges you can help them address?

Based on the conversations and your assessment of the results, begin the process of creating a "guiding coalition"[1] or steering committee. This can be formal or informal, depending on the culture of the company; but to be effective, this group must comprise senior stakeholder leaders who are:

- Known across the areas where you will have an impact
- Respected and trusted by their peers and subordinates
- Powerful, due to formal organizational authority or referential power, and able to make things happen
- Savvy about the formal and informal networks and operational models within the organization
- Willing to be your champions or mentors

This small team of supporters will provide both "air cover" and quiet counsel when necessary. Their most important value is the subtle guidance they can provide because they care about your success. In fact, they need you to succeed!

As you develop your 100-Day Plan, they are the ones who will review, augment, and approve it. They must be accessible and willing to lend their advice to the process. Too many senior executives offer to help but are too busy when needed. Their mentorship and guidance are a gauge of commitment to the procurement function.

1. Kotter, John P., *Leading Change*. Boston: Harvard Business Review Press, 2012.

Priority #2: You and Your Readiness to Lead

It is critical that value propositions be clarified.

First, the *functional* value proposition:

- Why did the organization decide to create or fill this position?
- What does Procurement need to do now to support the company?
- What is needed from Procurement in the future?
- What is the technology road map?
- Is funding available?
- How does the functional value proposition link to the company's strategic plan?

Second, your *personal* value proposition:

- Why did the organization select you?
- What did you say about yourself that resonated with the interview panel? As a functional leader? As a content leader? As a senior leadership team member?

The most effective procurement leaders we know did not leave their offices after accepting a new role without two to four hard-copy slides outlining (at a very high level) the value proposition for the procurement function. When they met somebody in the hallway or at a meeting who asked what they were doing and how Procurement was going to add value (or additional value), they had these support materials at the ready. This proactive anticipation of questions and readiness to enter the conversation on a personal level were incredibly effective and built trust rapidly with the stakeholder base. Compare this to the typical response of a quick conversation with the promise to "send an email with more information," and the value of a proactive, personal approach is readily apparent.

The Building Blocks of Content Excellence

Priority #3: Organizational Readiness and Capability

This is the ultimate "chicken-and-egg" situation. You must understand what is required from the organization to succeed; yet, you cannot promise results without first knowing the capability of the organization to deliver on its promises. Both must occur concurrently.

Start with the members of the procurement leadership team.

- Do they function well as a team?
- Are they capable of challenging and improving the current functional operating model?

- Are they currently structured logically?
- Do they understand their individual roles?
- Do they understand the procurement value proposition?
- How do they measure success?
- Do their functional measures align with how the company measures success?
- Are their measures credible with the broader stakeholder community?
- Do they understand the importance of stakeholder engagement, and can they demonstrate practical, effective application?

As individuals

- Are they capable procurement professionals in the core strategic competencies?
- Are they respected by their peers?
- Are they respected by their subordinates?
- Are they respected by their suppliers?

These questions (among others) will enable you to develop a plan to improve and align the functional leadership team. Ensuring that this team is speaking with one voice and is credible inside and outside of Procurement is one of your most important roles as its leader.[2]

We recommend carrying out a formal competency assessment using a third-party provider. The assessment should focus on staff development, as opposed to retention, and must be thorough and credible. To demonstrate leadership and courage, include yourself in this assessment. Once the picture of the leadership team is complete, do the same analysis with the balance of the sourcing organization. A formal competency assessment at the individual contributor level is best performed after you complete the leadership assessments. Based on firsthand experience, the leaders can answer natural questions from the participants. The trust established by "leader-first" behavior is invaluable.

Gaps in capability, performance, and trust are inevitable. Work with your Human Resources support team to develop plans for improvement in capability and performance. Trustworthiness, however, is rarely "coachable" and is best addressed by removing anyone deemed untrustworthy.

2. Lencioni, Patrick. *The Five Dysfunctions of a Team.* San Francisco: Jossey-Bass, 2002. Outlines the positive impacts (and negative consequences) of teams with clarity and consistency of messaging and priorities. It is an excellent, quick read and contains a number of practical exercises for real-world applications within a new or developing team.

There will also be pleasant surprises. The assessment will reveal capable and motivated people who are misplaced in the organization and represent a real opportunity to make a positive difference and demonstrate tangible leadership.

Finally, the quality of the spend data matters. Assess the ability to access current spend and planned-use data. Is the data "high-integrity" and accepted as valid on its face? Or is it, as in many organizations, limited to "directional use only" and deemed suspect, biased, or subject to verification. You will be making decisions based on the data and never want to be in a situation where you overpromise as result of suspect data. Trust but verify!

Pull It All Together

All of these assessments play into your 100-Day Plan. Use this information to develop plans to establish:

- Collaborative spend governance
- Sourcing and supplier-management processes
- Wave reviews
- Stage reviews
- Savings and value measurement

Each of these topics is covered fully in the subsequent pages.

Test your assessments early with your "guiding coalition." Do the members of your coalition see things the same way? If so, push forward. If not, ask them why not? Who is missing the kernel of what the assessments indicated as fact? If it is one of your advisors or mentors, then extreme care and careful education are warranted to ensure that you do not get too far out in front of this advisory group.

If it turns out that you are the one missing the complete picture, do a careful and thoughtful reappraisal. Go back to each question in this section and determine where you went off track. Talk to the members of your guiding coalition about this area. Talk to your personal network. Do not ignore this learning opportunity; if you do, this will surely be the cause of issues later.

The goal here is not to be negative or gloomy. The role of procurement leader is exciting on multiple fronts and is one of the more complex roles within the modern organization. A comprehensive view of the situation will position you for success. Good luck!

Chief Procurement Officer (CPO) Insights from Chris

The following template provides an excellent foundation and starting point, regardless of whether you are newly hired into an organization to evolve the procurement function or you were promoted from within the organization. Every leader has his/her own way of leading; now, you must lead and deliver on the expectations set by the executive team. You will also need to put your own imprint on the function. The important piece to remember, as you map out the plan, is that it must be sustainable, yet flexible enough to change as the direction of the business changes. If you are not open to change, you will not succeed.

In the nine years I've been Chief Procurement Officer (CPO), I've had four managers. I have had to make adjustments to the plan, and the functional organization has had to make changes. Expectations will always change; good enough is never good enough as you seek to deliver high-performance returns to the company. I sometimes set expectations too high; however, it gets me up in the morning to work in a role that is really stimulating.

TEMPLATE: 100-Day Plan, page 1

Assessment Parameter	Your Findings
1. What the company hired you to do or deliver	
2. Stakeholders a. Map and Key Priorities - Assurance of supply, Regulatory and ethical right to use, Quality, Service, Cost, and Innovation (A/RQSCI)	
3. Value Propositions a. Functional value proposition b. Your value proposition	
4. Organization Assessment a. Where is the function located (i.e., centrally, in a business unit, dispersed)? b. Why is it situated where it is? c. How good are the employees at the core elements of their roles? d. Does the organization have any allies? e. Does the organization have any potential enemies lurking in the weeds (organizationally and personally)?	
5. What must be delivered quickly (see #1 above)?	
6. Are there any current or emerging supply risks that must be addressed?	
7. What is your plan to ensure success?	
8. What support do you need in order to succeed? a. Internal b. External	
9. What is the ROI/business case?	

TEMPLATE: 100-Day Plan, page 2

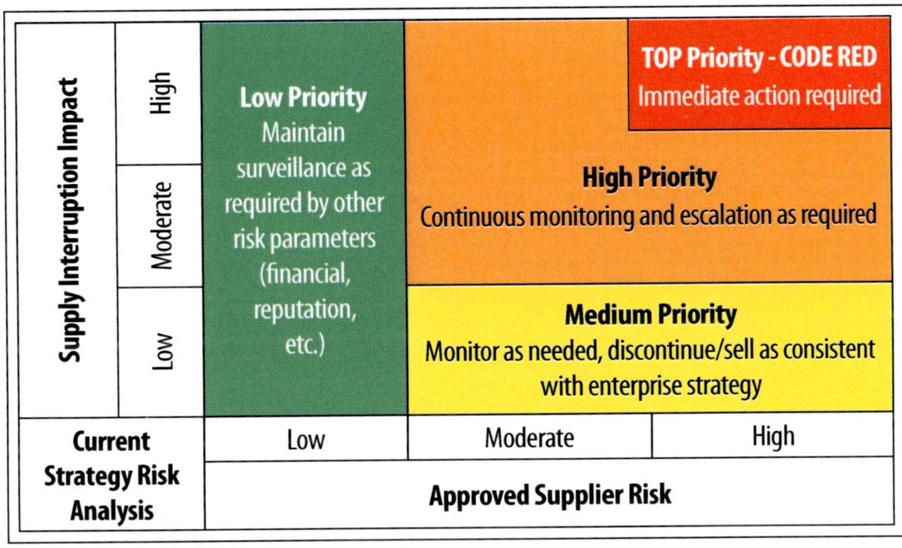

Current Strategy Risk Analysis

X-Axis: Approved Supplier Risk – The number of currently approved suppliers who are able to produce or supply in accordance with the current specifications

Y-Axis: Supply Interruption Impact – The severity of impact on the organization if the approved supply is interrupted or fails

Sole-source categories	
Sole-source rationale	
Who knows about the sole sourcing, and what are they saying?	
Inside Procurement	
Outside Procurement	
With whom and how will you share the risk insights?	
Names	**Methods & Core Messages**

2 Procurement Transformation Readiness Assessment

Topic Area Assessment Statements

Review these statements from your perspective as a procurement leader. If you "strongly agree" with all of the statements, you may wish to skip to the next topic. But, if you have some doubts about any of them, we recommend that you read this topic and engage in some self-reflection.

- Procurement leaders know and can access the overarching strategy goals of the company.
- The company's leadership works collaboratively and competes in a unified fashion against external rivals.
- The company has a comprehensive manufacturing strategy that incorporates the value from third-party suppliers.
- The company has a comprehensive research and development strategy that incorporates value from third-party suppliers.
- The company's leaders understand and appreciate the value of world-class procurement.
- The procurement function is ready to deliver world-class results to the broader organization.

Topic Introduction: Procurement Transformation Readiness Assessment

Many CEOs and CFOs want and need the results that Procurement can deliver to the company. That does not, however, equate to readiness to embrace world-class procurement.

World-class procurement is not merely making small improvements to the typical, tactically focused purchasing function. Processing purchase orders for stakeholders who preselected the suppliers (and agreed to all of the associated terms with the suppliers) is a low-value, clerical function. World-class procurement starts with early links to the strategic planning of the organization and is then proactively incorporated into the entire spectrum of business decision making.

Deployment of world-class procurement represents the pinnacle of procurement evolution and broader organizational maturity. Careful assessment of broader organizational readiness is required to ensure that the transformational journey is undertaken only in areas that are ready, willing, and able to sustain the effort through the required change processes.

The maturity of the procurement function in an organization reflects two variables: (1) the readiness of the broader organization to embrace the procurement value proposition, and (2) the ability of the function to deliver on that value proposition. The first step in the process is to understand the organization's readiness to embrace the future of Procurement.

Topic-Specific Nomenclature

As in every industry, procurement professionals use a range of language with very specific definitions. The following terms and definitions are used in this section:

- ***None***

The Tool: Procurement Transformation Readiness Assessment

Step 1 – Assess Procurement's progress along the transformation journey.

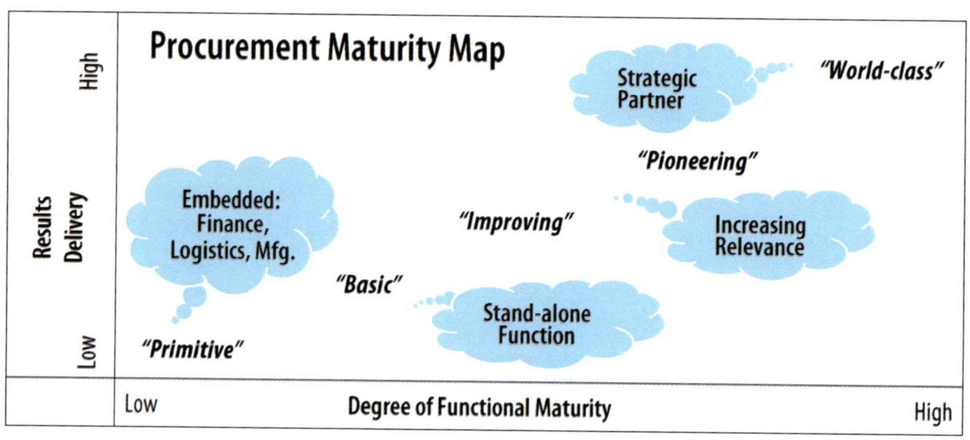

Typical stages in the procurement evolution are as follows:

- *Primitive* – Basic purchasing elements embedded in another department (e.g., Finance, Logistics, or Manufacturing) and engaged in direct procurement with the spending function
- *Basic* – Purchasing established as a stand-alone function
- *Improving* – Purchasing responsible for basic needs (e.g., transaction processing and service needs)
- *Pioneering (Category and supplier management implemented)* – Purchasing becomes an active participant in the spend governance process through cross-functional process application.
- *World-class* – Purchasing becomes a key element in delivery of corporate-strategy requirements in spend management/cost control, innovation, compliance, etc.

Note: Some practitioners chafe at the phrase "world-class," and it is overused in some circles. In this context it means those who are setting the bar, irrespective of industry or of leading-edge practices. If thinking about this level at the "leading or cutting edge" is more acceptable to you, please make the switch in your mind.

Using as much objective information as possible (stakeholder surveys, supplier surveys, external benchmarking, etc.), we suggest that you assess the current status of the procurement function. *Note: The responses are likely to vary by business unit and geography. The more detailed and specific the assessment, the more useful it will be in subsequent readiness assessments and change-planning sessions.*

The journey to world-class procurement is best viewed as a layered strategy, as in category strategies. However, Procurement cannot evolve or transform more quickly than the broader organization's readiness to adopt the changes.

Step 2 – Assess the readiness and need for procurement transformation.

At the business level you are considering for implementation (i.e., enterprise-wide, discrete business unit, corporate function, geographic unit, etc.), *assess the organizational leadership and documented business strategy* for the following key organizational parameters (all at the senior/pan-organizational-unit level).

It is critical to engage the most senior leadership, supported by Human Resources (or Organizational Development, depending on the HR structure), to make these assessments. This is an extraordinarily sensitive and confidential effort. Do not share the process or the results beyond those whom you know to be supportive of your efforts and are "airtight" with sensitive information.

Note: This is not a simple "desk assessment" to be done by Procurement alone but rather must occur as active dialogue that directly involves line and appropriate staff leaders.

The definitions, scales, and implications for each parameter are set forth below, with the goal being a frank assessment of each, followed by a tally that reflects all of the assessments and associated implications.

Business Strategy: the extent to which the organization has and follows a defined strategy to create marketplace success through sustainable product/service differentiation

Business Strategy Assessment	Implications for Procurement Transformation
Primitive – No strategy statement; "more of the same"	Procurement transformation will not succeed; it is not linked to the strategy.
Basic – An initial attempt at branding with no real uniqueness	Procurement transformation must be targeted and focused only on brand-related items.
Improving – Focus on low-cost production with no branding to build uniqueness or customer equity	Procurement transformation should focus on cost of goods sold (COGS) items and relatively easy indirect spends.
Pioneering – Focus on low-cost production with initial branding efforts	Procurement transformation should be broadly based on successful category management and broad stakeholder engagement; confirm that measurement schemes reflect the "voice of the customer."
World-class – Focus on low-cost production; branding actively linked with demonstrable uniqueness	Procurement transformation will result from "customer pull"; be certain that the implementation does not occur faster than can be successfully managed with current (or available) resources.

Market Urgency: the effects of outside forces on the culture and behavior of the business leaders and associates

Market Urgency Assessment	Implications for Procurement Transformation
None – No recognized pressure to change or improve (disconnected)	Procurement transformation (any procurement involvement) will not succeed; it is not viewed as necessary.
Low – Focused on competitive parity ("me too") efforts	Procurement transformation must focus narrowly on enhancing competitiveness of the key items.
Increasing – Facing commoditization of current products	Procurement transformation to focus on COGS issues related to the current product offerings.
Urgent – Viability of the business structure/organizational model in question	Procurement transformation should be focused on successful category management where a high-quality stream of quick wins is identified and rapidly implemented.
Do or Die – Current business model and products under siege from all corners	Procurement transformation will result from "customer pull"; emphasis on efforts to drive savings and future differentiation is the key to success.

R & D / Innovation Strategy: the ongoing plans and methods to sustain unique market offerings *(Note: Do not read into this parameter a skew toward product businesses; think of this broadly in terms of the business's approach to innovation regardless of the product or service lines.)*

R & D / Innovation Assessment	Implications for Procurement Transformation
Primitive – No innovation strategy	Procurement transformation (any procurement involvement) within R & D is viewed as unnecessary (and typically discouraged and prevented).
Basic – Solely in-house (dominated by "not-invented-here" fears)	Procurement transformation difficult in R & D; may succeed over time by developing a "preferred-supplier" listing.
Improving – Networked with outside; controlled inside to avoid any intellectual-property issues	Procurement transformation may expand; must develop functional expertise in key category areas, as well as intellectual-property contracting.
Pioneering – Networks with shared participation; intellectual-property issues surfacing for problem solving	Procurement transformation will include direct participation on new product/service development and scale-up teams; organizational readiness to support these requirements is key. Even without the "right person" at the helm, the innovation team will proceed.
World-class – Virtual with most capable participants, regardless of location and affiliation; intellectual-property issues fully addressed	Procurement transformation will result from "customer pull"; be certain that the implementation does not occur faster than can be successfully managed with current (or available) resources.

Spend Governance: the degree to which spend control is viewed as a "power" requirement versus a commercial opportunity

Spend Governance Assessment	Implications for Procurement Transformation
Primitive – Entire authority with stakeholders; no organized purchasing function	Procurement transformation (any procurement involvement) is not applicable.
Basic – Authority with stakeholders; Procurement involved in processing	Procurement transformation too early; establish credibility with processing, and push for results when given an opportunity.
Improving – Joint efforts to manage the spend and plan improvement efforts are initiated	Procurement transformation will expand; rely on shared-governance models and joint goal setting.
Pioneering – Procurement viewed as the expert and given authority to act on behalf of the business	Procurement transformation should be broadly based on shared governance and use of active stakeholder management throughout the category-management process to ensure continuous goal alignment.
World-class – Mutual; shared responsibility tangibly linked to the business strategy	Procurement transformation to start with the business-planning process and carry on throughout the product/service life cycle, including all aspects of the supply and value chain.

Functional Capability: the assessment of the function's progress along the improvement journey

Functional Capability Assessment	Implications for Procurement Transformation
Primitive – The function does not exist in any real sense.	Do not start procurement transformation. Develop the business case for initial implementation of the function.
Basic – Transactional approach only ("place and chase")	Develop capability to address high-priority categories and make all transactional systems operational.
Improving – Stakeholders set the requirements and determine the suppliers; procurement creates a final contract.	Procurement transformation can expand only if the stakeholder community (and business leadership) believes the commercial and market values delivered by procurement are justified. Build competence in both areas.
Pioneering – Procurement leads the management of strategic relationships and purchases in the supply chain.	Procurement transformation is poised for success and expansion; confirm that clear governance directs future activities, and internal competence is established in advance of stakeholder requirements.
World-class – Procurement is fully world class in making decisions and setting requirements throughout the supply chain	Procurement transformation is poised for success; make certain that measurement schemes fully reflect the voice of the customer and are embedded in mutual goal-development processes.

Supply Chain Integration: the role of internal and external supply chains

Supply Chain Integration Assessment	Implications for Procurement Transformation
Primitive – Completely separate approaches to internal and external finished-goods production to meet supply demands	Procurement transformation is premature; focus efforts at the unit level.
Basic – Initial sharing of productive capability inside the organization; little external awareness	Procurement transformation is premature; create appropriate market awareness, and build functional understanding of "lean" supply requirements.
Improving – Internal efforts are well coordinated; nascent "lean" implementation starting; evolving view of external capability	Procurement transformation poised for rapid expansion if functional staff can provide clear market insights and assurances of external capability; comprehensive understanding of "lean" supply is required.
Pioneering – "Lean" efforts are extensive internally and expanding to the supply base; conduct active review of internal and external capability before supply-chain decisions are made.	Procurement transformation now driven by an agreed-upon supply-chain strategy; measurements must be linked to the voice of the customer and reflect global best-practice benchmarks.
World-class – Supply chain viewed seamlessly and managed to rationally support market requirements; "lean" efforts in place throughout the supply chain regardless of internal or external location	Procurement transformation "pulled" by the supply-chain strategy and agreed-upon governance models; functional expertise and stature to manage strategic suppliers will determine long-term functional involvement.

Step 3 – Summarize and address the significant change-management issues.
Summarize the findings from Step 2. Each parameter will include a current-state readiness assessment and change-management implications. Once this summary is completed, review it with the steering board/committee/collaborative governance bodies to plan the path forward.

Note: Assessing the business strategy and sharing the findings involve sensitive information and may be controversial. Be certain that the presented content does not inordinately affect the feedback nor derail the process.

The outcome of the assessments will be an agreed-upon transformation plan that includes the key steps required to build organizational readiness:

- Inside the function
- Across the stakeholder community
- Across the supply base

Summary

The pace of procurement transformation reflects the readiness of the business and corresponding senior leaders to embrace the new procurement value proposition. Active change management is required to accelerate the adoption process. Remain vigilant during the process to ensure continued alignment and prevent discontent. Depending on the starting point of transformation and the degree of change, stakeholders may feel a loss of control and empowerment. Fill this void in a positive way by consciously building their trust in you and confidence in your team.

CPO Insights from Chris

The mission and organization of the procurement function are a reflection of the business leaders' readiness to embrace the procurement value proposition. As leaders understand and appreciate the value that Procurement can deliver, they will expect more. Additionally, as leaders focus on external, market-based competition and embrace internal collaboration, Procurement's ability to deliver results improves. This is an evolutionary process, which should be continually assessed to be sure you are able to meet the company's needs. Depending on the size and scale of the company, after interviewing key decision makers, you should ask yourself the following questions:

1. What are the top three to five areas in which you can build up trust for the function?
2. What does the end-to-end process look like?
3. What does the technology road map look like?
4. Are there any tax implications for the company that may cause it to move operations to different geographic areas to take advantage of lower taxes?

The Overarching Procurement Value Proposition

Organization: ____________________________

Successful procurement leaders use this approach to frame the procurement value proposition discussion with business leaders. Add the numbers for your company, and build the complete picture.

Suppliers	**Value (goods & services)** **Managed by:** **Initially** – *everyone (therefore, nobody)* **World-class** – *Stakeholders and Procurement agree on requirements, and Procurement determines the discrete value.*	**Your Company** **Total sales =** **$________** **Total third-party spend =** **$_______** Direct spend = $______ Indirect spend = $_______ Difference between sales & third-party spend = employees, taxes, shareholders, and plaintiffs	**Value (goods & services)** **Managed by:** **Marketing** *determines the offerings* **Sales** *determines the discrete value*	Customers

See next page, Underlying logic

Underlying logic of procurement value proposition:

Q: How much effort is focused on the "front" of the business?

A: Marketing and sales are integral to the company strategy. Much leadership attention and training efforts should be focused on these areas in order for the business to provide the products and services needed today and in the future.

Q: How much effort is focused on the "back" of the business?

A: Historically, much less. Spend-decision rights are widely distributed and commercial training (i.e., strategic sourcing, negotiations, supplier management, among others) is narrowly focused on procurement.

Q: What are the implications?

A: If it is important to optimize the value equation (value for money exchange) on the customer-facing side of the business, then it should be equally important on the supplier-facing side. In short, investing in Procurement is important to ensure the health and vitality of the enterprise.

3 Strategic Sourcing and Supplier Management Overview

Topic Area Assessment Statements

Review these statements from your perspective as a procurement leader. If you "strongly agree" with all of the statements, you may wish to skip to the next topic. But, if you have some doubts about any of them, we recommend that you read this chapter and engage in some self-reflection.

- My team uses a consistent process to achieve and maintain market parity in basic categories.
- My team employs a robust process to achieve competitive advantage in strategic categories.
- My team expects consistent strategic-sourcing process application across all managed categories.
- My team segments suppliers in a manner consistent with the category potential.
- My team manages suppliers in a manner consistent with the category segmentation.
- My team engages in consistent supplier-management process application.

Topic Introduction: Overview of Strategic Sourcing and Supplier Management

The strategic-sourcing (also known as the category-management) process is the end-to-end process used to:

- Address priority spend areas
- Understand current and future business requirements
- Understand supplier and supply-market information
- Conduct strategic analysis to derive strategic insights
- Develop a layered strategy
- Implement the strategy
- Launch appropriate supplier-management activities

Many companies deploy this process in one form or another and include five to seven steps. The key to success is to keep an open mind. Do not develop the strategy and then use the process to prove it is correct. Start with the category-value hypothesis from Chapter 4: Category Opportunity Assessment.

When you complete the assessment, you will have a hypothesis about what the category is worth from a value perspective and the anticipated avenues or approaches you might take to achieve that value. After that, allow intellectual curiosity and strategic analysis to reveal new possibilities.

Apply the most extensive use of the process across categories based on the underlying importance of the category to the business. The more strategic/critical the category is to the business, the greater the process rigor required.

Sourcing Strategies Address	Supplier-Management Strategies Address
• Category definition (what is included or what is "nearby" and excluded?) • Business requirements – now and into the future • Stakeholder analysis, including current spend-governance mapping • Supply-market analysis • Strategic analysis (using the applicable tools adjusted appropriately) • Risk analysis (strategy and implementation) • Layered-strategy development and change-leadership implications • Implementation plans, including pilots, broader rollout, compliance management, "how-to-buy" guides	• Category segmentation • Supplier segmentation • Current supplier performance • Stakeholder analysis, including spend-governance mapping • Supplier-relationship maps • Risk analysis (strategy and implementation) • Value-creation plans

Topic-Specific Nomenclature

As in every field, procurement professionals use a range of terminology with very specific definitions. The following terms and definitions are used in this section:

- ***Category/sub-category***–An area of spend with consistent goods or services and related supply base; defined in overall spend taxonomy; often based on UNSPSC coding or the equivalent
- ***Sponsor***–The stakeholder executive who is most interested in and linked to outcomes of the procurement process; often the senior budget holder

The Tool: Strategic Sourcing and Supplier Management Overview

The essential steps to execute the sourcing process are as follows:

Organizing the strategic-sourcing process into a set of discrete activities is the key to success. The cross-functional team members are counting on the procurement team leader to efficiently and effectively deploy the process and deliver the results. The following is a recommended flow of meetings and activities to achieve success.

Note: The process below should seamlessly follow the category launch/collaborative-governance-process steps.

Scope	Process Step	Participants	Venue(s)	Comments	Outputs
By Category Team	**Draft Team Charter**	Sourcing professional with sponsor input	Personal workstation and face-to-face	This process adds to the category opportunity assessment (milestones, value, rigor, etc.) and the team members.	Draft of team charter with required team members[1].
	Team Kick-Off	Sourcing professional (team leader), sponsor, and team members	Face-to-face	Team kick-off meetings are best conducted in person, but virtual meetings can work if the extent of probable change is modest. If the potential for substantive change exists, then face-to-face meetings are preferable. Sponsor is expected to attend the launch or kick-off, outline the goals for the team, and reiterate his personal commitment to the team.	• Team is assembled and ready to begin work. • Team reviews the charter and opportunity analysis. • Communication to key stakeholders by the team commences (teach charter content—scope, timing, participants, and how to provide input).

1. The Team Charter is to be reviewed by the area governance body (Steering Team) as needed. Reviews are typically focused on leveling resource utilization across team members and aligning personal objectives for individuals serving on the team with their departmental goals to ensure they are recognized and compensated for their team activities.

Scope	Process Step	Participants	Venue(s)	Comments	Outputs
By Category Team	**Data Analysis**	Sourcing professional and team members	Virtual (audio or video) conferencing (face-to-face as needed; typically multiple meetings)	Team to collect and review data. *Note: All data must be assessed for potential value before collection by the team, which should also agree in advance on the data collection to determine whether it can be used efficiently.*	• Strategic-insights development starts. • Communication with key stakeholders continues (focused on business-requirements development, emerging strategic insights, and team progress)
	Strategy Creation and Sponsor Review	Sourcing professional, team members, and sponsor	Face-to-face	Strategy creation meetings are the most difficult meetings in the process, particularly when the degree of change is substantial. Face-to-face meetings are highly recommended at the site of the most change-resistant stakeholder (factory or office location), if possible. We recommend using a dedicated facilitator. This is a difficult meeting to lead and facilitate. A peer in an unrelated category is ideal to support the category leader as an unbiased process facilitator.	• Draft layered strategy that is reviewed by the category sponsor. • Estimate value (A/RQSCI) and timing for the strategy. • Create, draft, and develop implementation budget (if necessary). • Change implementation difficulty, assessment, and recommendations (for a new implementation team, etc.). • Identify the required decision-makers to approve the strategy.

Scope	Process Step	Participants	Venue(s)	Comments	Outputs
By Category Team	**Strategy Approval**	Sponsor, team, team leader, and key stakeholders	Face-to-face (may be multiple meetings)	Inform the area governance board of the progress; board will exercise its decision-making rights as appropriate. Convene additional meetings to obtain the balance of approvals necessary to proceed.	• Strategy approved with all change enablers (budgets, staff resources, etc.); agreed upon and in place, such as travel budgets, line trials, communications, team members.
	Strategy Implementation	Sourcing professional, sponsor, and team	Varies; may be more than one	Implementation of a layered category strategy often occurs over years and includes many tasks and projects. It is critical to maintain momentum, identify and implement quick wins along the way, and ensure that all of the discrete activities are aligned and consistent with the overall strategy.	• Strategic value realization (A/RQSCI)

Supplier Management Overview

Do not start with supplier segmentation. Start with category segmentation, and then segment suppliers based on the underlying categories they supply. This will ensure a focus on the critical few suppliers who are supporting the key categories.

The first step in effective supplier management is to review strategic-analysis results and ***identify the most important spend categories.*** Focus on the critical few categories for the future, including the categories that:

- Will yield product and process innovations and secure the future of the firm
- Include critical risk issues
- Address the significant outsourced "backroom" activities

These areas of focus should be laser sharp to permit adequate allocation of time. There are literally tens of thousands of suppliers for large firms, but the success of the company depends on alignment with very few. Identify them, and give them your support.

The following process summary uses two core tools from strategic sourcing and is very successful at identifying the key categories of spend:

Lean Portfolio:

- **Strategic** – Focus on innovation (product or service) with the potential to differentiate the company in the marketplace—*highest priority.*
- **Lean** – Focus on process innovation—*high priority.*
- **Critical** – Focus on assurance of supply to guarantee continuity of operations—*high priority.*
- **Leverage** – Focus on cost—*exceptions only.*
- **Acquisition** – Focus on process efficiency—*exceptions only.*

<table>
<tr><td rowspan="3">Market Difficulty / Supply Risk</td><td>High</td><td rowspan="2">Critical
High Priority</td><td>Strategic
Highest Priority</td></tr>
<tr><td>Moderate</td><td>Lean
High Priority</td></tr>
<tr><td>Low</td><td>Acquisition
Exceptions Only</td><td>Leverage
Exceptions Only</td></tr>
<tr><td colspan="2" rowspan="2">Lean Portfolio</td><td>Low</td><td>High</td></tr>
<tr><td colspan="2">Profit/Spend Impact</td></tr>
</table>

Category Segmentation:

- **Custom** – Focus on innovation (product/service) with the goal of differentiation—*highest priority.*
- **Tailored** – Focus on process innovation/service (often an outsourced capability)—*high priority.*
- **Proprietary** – Focus on assurance of supply to ensure continuity of operations—*high priority.*
- **Generic** – Focus on cost—*exceptions only.*

<table>
<tr><td rowspan="2">Number of Sellers with Access to Intellectual Property</td><td>More than one (>1)</td><td>Tailored
High Priority</td><td>Generic
Exceptions Only</td></tr>
<tr><td>One</td><td>Custom
Highest Priority</td><td>Proprietary
High Priority</td></tr>
<tr><td colspan="2" rowspan="2">Category Segmentation</td><td>One</td><td>More than one (>1)</td></tr>
<tr><td colspan="2">Number of Customers</td></tr>
</table>

The final step is to align the insights from both tools to produce a comprehensive view.

Lean Portfolio	**Likely Supplier Segmentation**	**Category Segmentation**
Strategic	Strategic suppliers	Custom
Lean	Key suppliers	N/A
Critical	Key suppliers (at-risk supply)	Proprietary
Leverage	Base suppliers	Tailored (base and key suppliers)
Acquisition	Approved/base suppliers	Generic

The great news in this analysis is that *typically 70 percent +/- of the spend categories can be objectively placed in the generic and the leverage/acquisition quadrants.* They may not start there based on current behavior, but this is where they objectively belong. Once you achieve consistent marketplace leverage through strategy implementation and change management, focus on the critical suppliers to unlock the underlying specifications and build a case for change.

When you have segmented the spend categories, it is possible to segment suppliers based upon the categories they supply. There is no correct number of segmentation levels, and we see schemes ranging from three to five (or more!). We recommend four, which enables a focus on the critical few and avoids consuming too much time on the segmentation process itself.

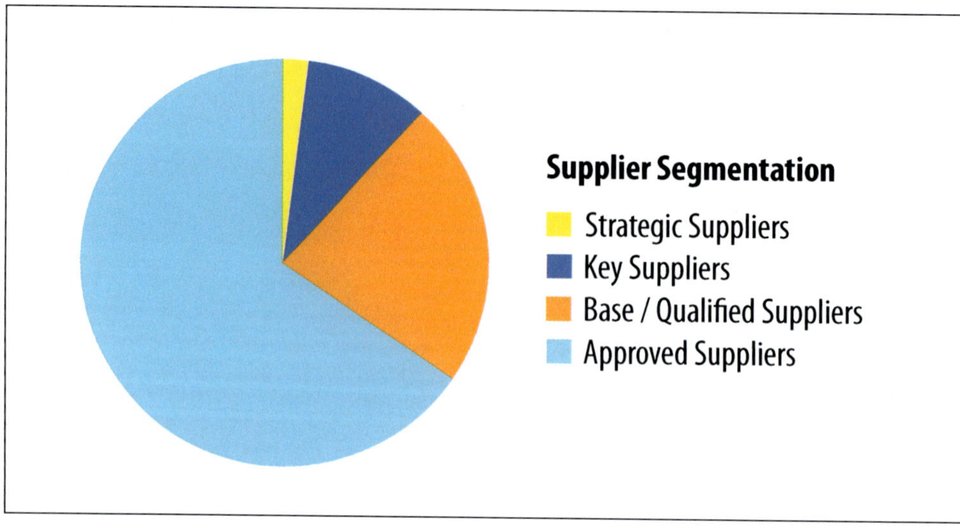

- **Strategic Suppliers –** The critical few *(typically fewer than ten for the entire company)* with which the company will share extensive information and create new and differentiated offerings; must be characterized by a mutually beneficial relationship. This produces a true win-win.
- **Key Suppliers –** Suppliers who are critical to both the efficiency of current operations and the ongoing supply of goods and services
- **Base/Qualified Suppliers –** Suppliers who are fully vetted (quality, systems, finances, Tier 2/3 supply chains for 3TG, etc.) and supply current operations
- **Approved Suppliers –** The lowest level that support simple, recurring operations

Note: A strategic supplier meets all of the criteria for strategy and the levels below; the requirements are cumulative as the segmentation moves to higher levels.

Many companies document the category- and supplier-segmentation processes using spreadsheets with agreed-upon criteria. These are excellent guides, but the results must be verified to be certain that the applied criteria are appropriate and the results are credible. Too often, the "criticality of supply" is overweighted, and simple packaging components (base category and approved suppliers) are mislabeled "strategic" as a result. On the next two pages is an excellent example that works extremely well in practice.

The first step in the process is to confirm the category-segmentation level. How important is the spend category to the future of the firm? To continuing operations?

The example below is an excellent Excel-based system. We see many systems that are computer based and contain faulty logic. An impressive visual result does not replace bad thinking. Get the thinking right, and then explore automation. A Becton Dickinson strategic-sourcing manager, Anirban Mukherjee, as a developmental assignment, created this example. It is a wonderful illustration of what a really smart, capable sourcing professional can do—something that a staff person without the context of the actual work would be unlikely to create.

The example demonstrates the breadth of strategic thinking necessary to assess the supplier's tactical fit and broader compatibility with the buying firm. The supplier may be an excellent niche supplier, but if the needs are extensive and global, is it the right strategic fit? Proper criteria help limit the impact of subjectivity on the assessment process.

Category or Subcategory:	
Desired Category Segmentation Level:	

	Strategic Fit/Compatibility												
CRITERIA:	Suppliers capability to meet Company's current and Future Business Requirements		Current Relationship between Company and Supplier		Alignment with Company's Strategies and Business Goals		Supplier motivation and willingness to collaborate and share		Cultural and Geographic Fit		Commercial Power Assessment (Company Power vs. Supplier Power vs. Evenly Matched		Strategic Fit/ Compatibility Score
WEIGHT:	40%		20%		10%		10%		10%		10%		100%
SCORING	1 = Not consistently meeting, 5 = Meets current/Future questionalble, 10 = Meets or exceed current/Capable to meet future		1 = Strained - viewed as Nusiance or Exploitable, 3 = Improving - viewed as Nusiance or Exploitable, 5 = viewed as Development or Core, 10 = viewed as Development or Core with a strong current relationship		1 = No alignment or understanding, 5 = Some understanding with potential for alignment, 10 = Fully aware, understands and aligned		1 = No Motivation, 5 = Demonstrates some motivation and willingness, 10 = High Motivated -actively collaborates/ shares		1 = Limited fit, 10 = Strong fit		1 = Supplier Power, 5= Company Power, 10 = Evenly Matched		
Name	Assessment	Score	Assessment	Score	Assessment	Score	Assessment	Score	Assessment	Score	Assessment	Score	Total Score
A	10.0	40.0	10.0	20.0	5.0	5.0	10.0	10.0	1.0	1.0	10.0	10.0	86.0
B	10.0	40.0	10.0	20.0	5.0	5.0	10.0	10.0	1.0	1.0	10.0	10.0	86.0
C	10.0	40.0	10.0	20.0	5.0	5.0	10.0	10.0	1.0	1.0	10.0	10.0	86.0
D	10.0	40.0	10.0	20.0	5.0	5.0	10.0	10.0	10.0	10.0	10.0	10.0	95.0
E	10.0	40.0	10.0	20.0	5.0	5.0	10.0	10.0	10.0	10.0	10.0	10.0	95.0
F	5.0	20.0	5.0	10.0	5.0	5.0	5.0	5.0	1.0	1.0	10.0	10.0	51.0
G	5.0	20.0	10.0	20.0	5.0	5.0	10.0	10.0	10.0	10.0	10.0	10.0	75.0
H	5.0	20.0	10.0	20.0	5.0	5.0	10.0	10.0	1.0	1.0	10.0	10.0	66.0
I	5.0	20.0	10.0	20.0	5.0	5.0	10.0	10.0	1.0	1.0	10.0	10.0	66.0
J	5.0	20.0	10.0	20.0	5.0	5.0	5.0	5.0	1.0	1.0	10.0	10.0	61.0
		0.0		0.0		0.0		0.0		0.0		0.0	0.0
		0.0		0.0		0.0		0.0		0.0		0.0	0.0
		0.0		0.0		0.0		0.0		0.0		0.0	0.0
		0.0		0.0		0.0		0.0		0.0		0.0	0.0
		0.0		0.0		0.0		0.0		0.0		0.0	0.0

Growth and Value Drivers												
Supplier Impact on Current and Future Revenue; Risk Profile		Supplier Innovation		Supplier Value Improvement and Creation Capability		Growth Potential		Cost Transparency		Supplier Performance		Growth and Value Drivers Score
10%		30%		20%		10%		10%		20%		100%
1 = High Risk/No contingency, 5 = Low to Medium Risk/Contingency plan in place, 10 = Low/No Risk-Response plan in place		1 = No evidence of innovation/capability, 5 = Occasional attempts/offerings put forth by supplier, 10 = Readily demonstrates and helps plan and implement innovation and value creation programs		1 = No evidence of value creation, 5 = Occasional attempts/offerings put forth by supplier, 10 = Readily demonstrates and helps plan and implement value creation programs		1 = No Potential, 5 = Some potential, but would require investment in infrastructure, 10 = Currently positioned to support growth opportunities		1 = No Transparency - Closed book approach, 5 = Provides information on a limited basis, data not always complete, 10 = Open book approach - looks for ways to increase value delivery through reduced costs		1 = Overall Performance Rating of < 80%; 5 = Overall Performance Rating > 80 <90%; 10 = Overall Performance Rating ≥ 90% -- **NOTE: *Lowest evaluation score from supplier/supplier site should be reflected here.***		
Assessment	Score	Assessment	Score	Assessment	Score	Assessment	Score	Assessment	Score	Assessment	Score	Total Score
10.0	10.0	10.0	30.0	10.0	20.0	5.0	5.0	5.0	5.0	1.0	2.0	72.0
10.0	10.0	10.0	30.0	10.0	20.0	5.0	5.0	5.0	5.0	1.0	2.0	72.0
10.0	10.0	5.0	15.0	10.0	20.0	5.0	5.0	5.0	5.0	0.0	0.0	55.0
10.0	10.0	5.0	15.0	5.0	10.0	5.0	5.0	5.0	5.0	0.0	0.0	45.0
10.0	10.0	5.0	15.0	5.0	10.0	5.0	5.0	5.0	5.0	0.0	0.0	45.0
10.0	10.0	5.0	15.0	1.0	2.0	5.0	5.0	5.0	5.0	0.0	0.0	37.0
10.0	10.0	5.0	15.0	5.0	10.0	5.0	5.0	5.0	5.0	0.0	0.0	45.0
10.0	10.0	5.0	15.0	5.0	10.0	5.0	5.0	5.0	5.0	0.0	0.0	45.0
10.0	10.0	5.0	15.0	5.0	10.0	5.0	5.0	5.0	5.0	0.0	0.0	45.0
10.0	10.0	5.0	15.0	1.0	2.0	5.0	5.0	5.0	5.0	0.0	0.0	37.0
	0.0		0.0		0.0		0.0		0.0		0.0	0.0

The second step is to outline the assessment criteria. In this example, the discrete criteria are segregated by the macro headings of "Strategic Fit/Compatibility" and "Growth and Value Drivers." The criteria you select must be validated taking into consideration the broader business requirements.

The discrete criteria are then used to assess the current capability of the supplier. Objective criteria must be used and fully defined, as in this example. Note the use of clear and defensible criteria-evaluation parameters. This is excellent practice!

The value of the automation is to ensure the accuracy and completeness of the scoring and plotting.

Growth and Value Drivers	Strategic Fit/ Compatibility	Upper Right	Upper Left	Lower Right	Lower Left	Current Supplier Segmentation Level	Alignment (RAG)
72	86	1	-	-	-	Conventional	G
72	86	1	-	-	-	Conventional	G
55	86	1	-	-	-	Conventional	G
45	95	-	1	-	-	Conventional	G
45	95	-	1	-	-	Conventional	G
37	51	-	1	-	-	Conventional	G
45	75	-	1	-	-	Conventional	G
45	66	-	1	-	-	Conventional	G
45	66	-	1	-	-	Conventional	G
37	61	-	1	-	-	Conventional	G
-	-	-	-	-	1	-	
-	-	-	-	-	1	-	
-	-	-	-	-	1	-	
-	-	-	-	-	1	-	
-	-	-	-	-	1	-	

Alignment	Definition
RED	Supplier Assessment level is 2 levels below category positioning: Requires rigorous performance improvement program with specific time limits imposed. Failure to achieve required improvements will likely result in supplier change.
AMBER	Supplier Assessment level is 1 level below category positioning: Establish development program to achieve alignment.
GREEN	Supplier Assessment matches or exceeds category positioning: Proceed with appropriate level of engagement.

In this example, the growth/value drivers and strategic fit/compatibility criteria, versus the supplier's segmentation level, are assessed using an RAG scale.

Clarity on all scales—even as seemingly simple as red-amber-green (RAG)—is imperative so that all participants are aligned on the interpretation of the results. This RAG assessment highlights the suppliers who are below the requisite category requirements and those who meet the requirements.

The final step is to plot all of the suppliers against the requisite category segmentation. The resulting plot shows the fit of the suppliers versus the category requirements. It is an excellent visual depiction of the challenges facing the supplier management and development team.

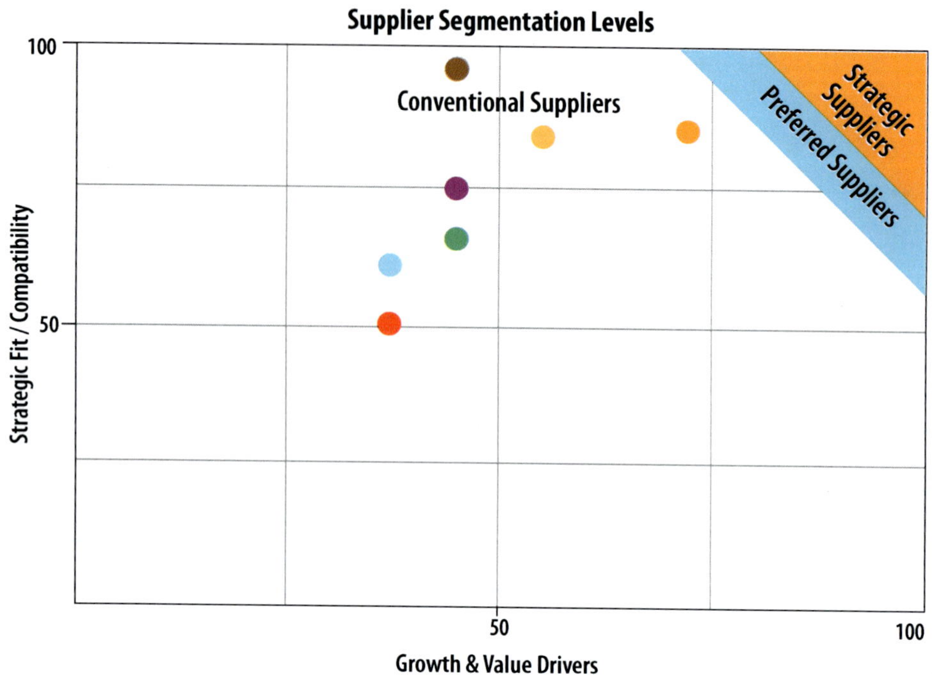

In this example, there are no strategic or preferred suppliers; all emerge as conventional suppliers (using the host organization's supplier-segmentation nomenclature).

Summary

Consistent application of the strategic-sourcing and supplier-management processes is required to achieve world-class procurement performance. This is the foundation for all other activities. Use of these processes:

- Enables access to preferred supplier-based innovations and service
- Ensures parity in commodity markets
- Confirms that the organization understands the supply markets and behaves in a way that maximizes its position in the markets

Focus on these processes requires a clear delineation between tactical and strategic activities. Absent this distinction, the business will inevitably push the procurement team into supporting the tactical day-to-day activities and diluting the functional value proposition.

CPO Insights from Chris

Sustaining value delivery is a challenge you will face as head of a procurement function. You do not want to be known as the "price chief" or the "contract king." As the head of Procurement, you must be seen as contributing true value to the company. Applying a robust sourcing methodology that engages cross-functional teams across a category of spend is one way to sustain the value and build trust with the stakeholder community.

The strategic sourcing process is a fact-based methodology facilitated by strong procurement professionals. It is a team sport and should not be seen as driven by Procurement with purchase price as the primary goal. To be credible and to establish strong alignment, the process must be collaborative; its analysis should include broad insights about the internal requirements and the external supply market. The process should also challenge the status quo and highlight opportunities for the future. It should recognize the opportunities and constraints associated with the current spend profile and portray a compelling view of the future.

However, the strategic sourcing process should also be thought provoking and engaging; it cannot accept the status quo as the correct way of moving forward in order for the stakeholders to see the potential value. The importance of a strong executive sponsor for each of the categories of spend is critical for success. The tendency is often to jump to the solution rather than reflecting on the facts. A sound decision will be made when all the facts are analyzed.

4 Category Opportunity Assessment

Topic Area Assessment Statements

Review these statements from your perspective as a procurement leader. If you "strongly agree" with all of the statements, you may wish to skip to the next topic. But, if you have some doubts about any of them, we recommend that you read this chapter and engage in some self-reflection.

- My team and I understand and document current internal category practices.
- My team and I understand and document leading-edge category practices.
- My team and I understand current and historical change constraints.
- My team and I know the potential value by category.

Topic Introduction: Category Opportunity Assessment

Opportunity analysis is one of the most important aspects of procurement leadership. Understanding the spend categories, historical and current practices, and future needs of the business shapes the approaches you will use to manage the function and prioritize resources.

Assessing opportunities includes direct stakeholder involvement through the collaborative spend governance process. Assessing categories, however, is the "homework" Procurement must do to inform the joint-governance process.

The category-opportunity assessment process includes both internal and relevant external assessment data. The goal is to compare "what is" with the practices of leading-edge category users to paint a picture of "what could be." The goal is *not* to dictate a mechanistic adoption of supposed "best practices" but rather to *paint the picture of what is possible.*

The results of the category-opportunity assessment are to be shared with stakeholders. This is part of the trust-building and joint-visioning process. As you engage with stakeholders, be on the lookout for the following situations:

- Most stakeholders are entirely focused on "what is" and may be blindsided by or resistant to believing that the "what-could-be/leading-edge" practices are possible. Leading-edge practices should be in place at specifically named organizations that can be contacted as references.

- Some stakeholders may be personally affected by the results (e.g., the leading-edge practices could include outsourcing of areas that directly affect them or their people, so use discretion, where appropriate, when you share insights.

The results of the category-opportunity assessment constitute a hypothesis, not a final strategy. The hypothesis will include an estimate of value (A/RQSCI, see chapter 7), necessary time to completion, required resources, and key change enablers. But it is *still* a hypothesis. It is the work of the team you select to develop the complete strategy and associated details.

Topic-Specific Nomenclature

As in most industries, procurement professionals use a range of terminology with very specific definitions. The following terms and definitions are used in this section:

- ***Change constraints:*** All current practices, beliefs, policies, and procedures that restrict changes in the supply base. Typical examples include restrictive and company-specific specifications instead of functional specifications, extended validation or registration procedures, and stakeholder beliefs that all changes introduce needless risk.
- ***Associate:*** Employee; can be inside or outside the procurement function.

The Tool: Category Opportunity Assessment

Procurement and key stakeholders should jointly develop the following information. The completed assessment is an important input to the collaborative spend-governance process (see chapter 5).

1. Understand what is occurring in your company.

Develop a comprehensive internal view of the facts and data for the category, including the answers to the following questions:

- Where/how are the goods/services in the category used?
- What is the current sourcing strategy?
- What is the current supply-strategy risk assessment?
- What are the current and projected volumes?
- Who are the current suppliers?
- What is the current performance level of the suppliers?
- How many transactions are processed for this category now?
- How are they processed, and what is the total transaction cost?

Develop a corresponding view of the change limits/enablers for the category, including the answers to the following questions:

- What are the unique characteristics of the company that dictate current practices?
- What is the overall product/service design?
- What are the specifications?
- What are the quality/regulatory practices?
- What are the beliefs/behaviors?

2. Understand what is occurring in companies that are regarded as world-class consumers of the category.

Develop a comprehensive internal view of the facts and data for the category, including the answers to the following questions:

- Who are the leading-edge consumers of this category (i.e., by name, which companies are regarded as the "best-practice" buyers/consumers of the category)?
- How did you identify the leading-edge users (sources), and how will you stay current with this information?
- What volume are they consuming?
- Who are their suppliers?
- What is the current performance level of their suppliers?
- What is the future of this category at leading-edge companies?

Develop a corresponding external view of the change limits/enablers for the category, including the answers to the following questions:

- What is distinct, unique, or special at the leading-edge firms that contributes to their performance?
- What is their overall product/service design?
- What are their specifications?
- What are their quality/regulatory practices?
- What are their beliefs/behaviors?

Develop a hypothesis for the category.
What is the estimated value that can be achieved if the company is able to advance current practices in terms of:

- Assurance of supply and regulatory/ethical right to use
- Quality
- Service
- Cost
- Innovation

How long will it take to achieve this value?

Describe the future state in terms of key parameters *without* explaining how to achieve the future state.

3. Develop a plan to move forward.
Who is best positioned to enable/support the changes?

- Headquarters
- Key consuming locations
- Other enablers

What are the recommended actions? They may include:

- Sharing the results with key stakeholders
- Chartering a category-strategy team

Summary

Engaging stakeholders in the process of jointly envisioning the future of third-party supply is an exciting and challenging process. It is the cornerstone of world-class procurement and requires substantial preliminary work and discipline. Objectively assessing current practices and comparing them to leading-edge practices allows you to create a value hypothesis to discuss with stakeholders. This is the foundation of collaborative-spend governance and a building block in the ongoing trust-building process.

CPO Insights from Chris

What is possible? Your role as a leader should be to consider leading-edge practices. As you build capability, you will develop associates who can look ahead and push your company to think outside the box. The more mature the organization becomes, the greater the need to consider possibilities that will challenge the business's thinking. The timing of these challenges comes down to the company's readiness for substantive change, the degree of trust present in the stakeholder community, and the capability of the procurement employee base to lead change. You do not want to overpromise and underdeliver due to capability gaps. Opportunity analysis is a critical process in building the business case and trust with internal stakeholders. Opportunity analysis should feed the dialogue with customers regarding the near-, mid-, and long-term plans for category strategy development.

TEMPLATE: Category Opportunity Assessment, page 1

Category Name – Functional Purpose –		
"Inside" Situation	***Inside the Company***	***Inside Constraints / Enablers***
	• Where/how are the goods/services in the category used? • What is the current sourcing strategy? • What is the current supply-strategy risk assessment? • What are the current and projected volumes? • Who are the current suppliers? • What is the current performance level of the suppliers? • How many transactions are processed for this category now? • How are they processed, and what is the total transaction cost?	What are the company's unique characteristics that dictate current practices: • Overall product/service design? • Specifications? • Quality/regulatory practices? • Beliefs/behaviors?
"Outside" Situation	***Across Leading-edge Category Users***	***Leading-edge Enablers***
	• Who are the leading-edge consumers of this category (i.e., by name, which companies are regarded as the "best-practice" buyers/consumers of the category)? • How did you identify the leading-edge users (sources), and how will you stay current with this information? • What volume are they using? • Who are their suppliers? • What is the current performance level of their suppliers? • What is the future of this category?	What is distinctive or unique at the leading-edge firms that enables their performance? • Overall product/service design • Specifications • Quality/regulatory practices • Beliefs/behaviors

TEMPLATE: Category Opportunity Assessment, page 2

<table>
<tr><td colspan="3">Category Name –
Functional Purpose –</td></tr>
<tr><td rowspan="2">Target</td><td colspan="2">Hypothesis</td></tr>
<tr><td>What is the estimate of value that can be achieved if the company is able to advance current practices in terms of:
• Assurance of supply & regulatory/ethical right to use?
• Quality?
• Service?
• Cost?
• Innovation?
How long will it take to achieve this value?</td><td>Describe the future state in terms of key parameters without explaining how to achieve the future state.</td></tr>
<tr><td rowspan="2">Proposal</td><td>Change Enablers</td><td>Proposed Actions</td></tr>
<tr><td>Who is best positioned to enable/support the changes:
• Headquarters?
• Key consuming locations?
• Other enablers?
Who are their suppliers?
What is the current performance level of their suppliers?
What is the future of this category?</td><td>Recommended actions include:
• Sharing the results with key stakeholders
• Chartering a category-strategy team</td></tr>
</table>

5 Collaborative Spend Governance

Topic Area Assessment Statements

Review these statements from your perspective as a procurement leader. If you "strongly agree" with all of the statements, you may wish to skip to the next topic. But, if you have some doubts about any of them, we recommend that you read this chapter and engage in some self-reflection.

- My team and I collaboratively plan and prioritize improvement efforts across spend categories with stakeholders.
- Appropriate business leaders sponsor the sourcing-strategy development teams.
- Appropriate cross-functional team members staff the sourcing-strategy teams.
- Stakeholders know and support strategy implementation and the associated change-leadership requirements.
- Stakeholders and Procurement jointly identify and agree on the most important categories.
- Stakeholders and Procurement jointly identify and agree on the required value by category (A/RQSCI).
- Stakeholders and Procurement jointly identify and agree on the time frame for value delivery.
- Stakeholders and Procurement jointly review and modulate process rigor to ensure an efficient, effective team process.

Topic Introduction: Collaborative Spend Governance

Successful procurement organizations understand that ultimate responsibility for spend and budget management always rests with the stakeholders; it is their budget. World-class organizations recognize this and exploit the added value of procurement to ensure that all spend is professionally managed. Establishing collaborative spend governance is the way to achieve these goals.

Selecting the critical few categories for strategy development is difficult. Usually, it is a procurement-driven process that focuses on the high-spend categories with the belief that this will yield the most value for the business (narrow, savings-biased approach). We recommend a more nuanced approach that is Procurement-led and requires close collaboration with business leaders to jointly agree on the categories that will yield the most current and future value (broad, inclusive approach).

Focus on the most important categories early, and extensively engage stakeholders in order to align the stakeholders' priorities with the potential opportunities identified in the category-opportunity assessment process. Once the priority categories are agreed upon, the work of improvement can begin. The category-launch process will answer the following key questions:

- Which are the most important categories and why?
- What is the potential value (A/RQSCI) that may be delivered?
- When will the estimated value be realized?
- Who is the appropriate sponsor for this effort?
- Who are the appropriate team members for this effort?
- What is the correct process rigor to apply to this effort?

The governance body for collaborative-spend governance is a steering body (typically a "council"). This can be:

- At the functional level for discrete, indirect spend areas (e.g., HR, Finance, Legal, Marketing, plant indirect, etc.)
- At the overarching level for direct areas (all spend categories related to a range of products or manufacturing) or geographies/business unit (all direct and indirect spend categories related to a country/region/business unit).
- For capital spend categories

The desired outcome is that participating stakeholders will possess the decision-making authority to engage in the processes from inception through implementation and fully enjoy the results they achieve.

These are vital questions whose answers will determine whether the resulting team is correctly slotted in the overall wave plan and poised for success. The process for migrating from the current state to professionally managed spends is by way of successive "waves" of improvement through the categories.

Topic-Specific Nomenclature

As in most industries, procurement professionals use a range of terminology with specific definitions. The following terms and definitions are used in this section:

- ***A/RQSCI*** – The complete range of potential business requirements for any category of spend: **A**ssurance of supply, **R**egulatory and ethical right to use, **Q**uality, **S**ervice, **C**ost, and **I**nnovation.
- ***Wave Plan*** – A plan that lists subsequent waves or groupings of category-team-launch efforts; jointly created with stakeholders to reflect mutual, agreed-upon business priorities.

The Tools: Steering Teams and Wave Planning

Steering Team

At the outset of a procurement-transformation initiative, we strongly recommend the establishment of an initiative-wide steering body (council) to govern the entire spend-governance process, as well as additional steering bodies to address the discrete issues associated with various areas and constituencies. If a steering body is not formed, you will not have the ability to address business-wide change implications.

Wave Plan

Wave planning is the process of sequencing the priority teams in a cadence the procurement function can lead and the stakeholders can support (i.e., they can afford the time and opportunity cost of the cross-functional team members). The prioritization of the teams must be expressly linked to overarching business requirements and specific stakeholder business plans.

Wave planning should go as quickly as possible without overwhelming either the procurement team's ability to lead the effort or the stakeholders' capacity to staff the teams with cross-functional team members. It is always possible to add teams to successful efforts, but it is tremendously demoralizing to re-launch a failed effort.

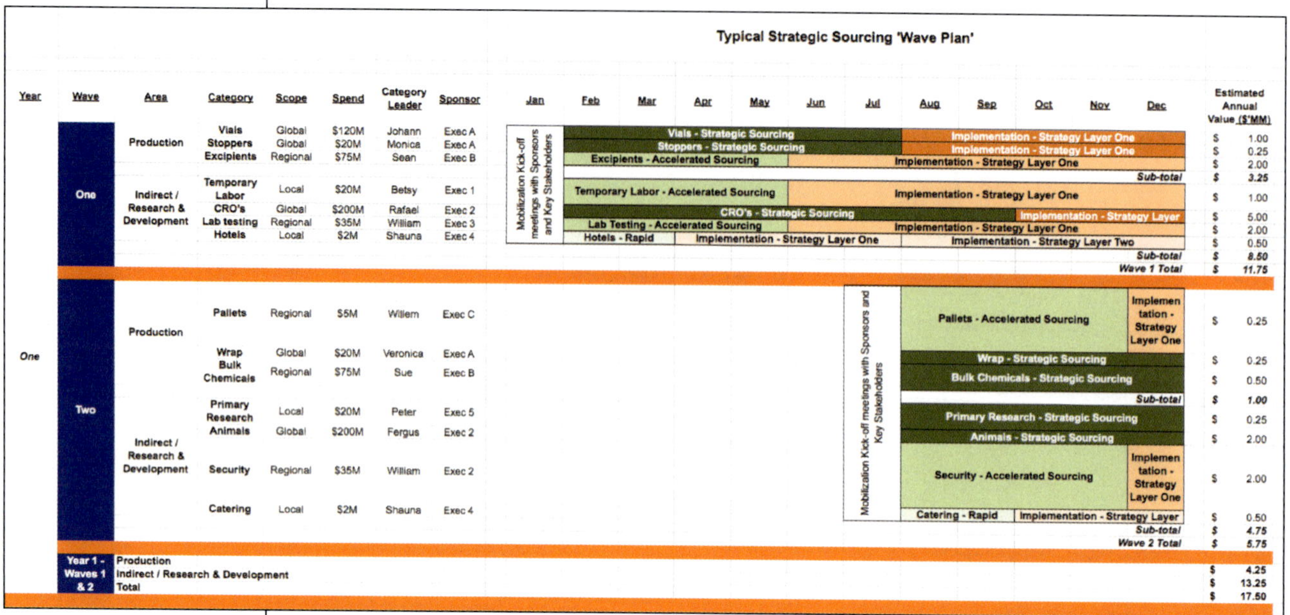

The detailed planning and engagement process necessary to achieve this progress is outlined below.

Category Launch Process

There are three steps in addressing the core issues in order to establish collaborative-spend governance with stakeholders. The following chart outlines, in detail, the process for executing the collaborative-spend governance process.

Scope	Process Step	Participants	Venue(s)	Comments	Outputs
Aligned by Stakeholder Interest Area (i.e. direct materials, capital, sub-sets of indirect by functional area)	**Draft Category – Opportunity Assessment**	Sourcing professional and procurement leader(s) with support from peers, stakeholders, and procurement leadership	Personal workstation	This is the core prep work necessary to understand the current situation in which the "better-practice" companies are engaged and the historical change environment. This is a hypothesis of potential category value—the associated business case for change and the rationale for investing team time and resources.	• Hypothesis of potential category value (A/RQSCI) • Change-readiness assessment
	Procurement Review	Sourcing professionals and procurement leader(s)	Face-to-face meeting (in person or virtual)	At this stage, the procurement leader(s) review the underlying work to be certain that it is rigorous, consistently performed across categories, and does not miss any key issues they may know of due to their unique perspectives.	• Draft category-opportunity assessments ready for review with applicable stakeholders
	Senior Stakeholder / Procurement Review	Affected senior stakeholders; procurement leaders *Note: Sourcing professionals may be included if they will not cause a chilling effect on the conversations. Too many people at widely divergent seniority levels often lead to cautious and stilted conversations. These conversations must be open and frank.*	Face-to-face (much better in-person but can be virtual if necessary)	This process establishes the ongoing collaborative-spend governance and must be focused. The categories discussed should be relevant to the stakeholders; hold as many meetings as necessary to be sure that they are.	• Agreed-upon prioritization of categories • Confirmed hypotheses of value (A/RQSCI) and delivery timing • Designated team sponsor • Anticipated process-rigor assessment • Team budget (travel, line trials, etc., as applicable and needed)

Summary

Engaging stakeholders and establishing collaborative-spend governance is a foundation-level activity for procurement and stakeholders. These efforts set the agenda and the tenor for the relationship between Procurement and the stakeholders. Jointly envisioning the future of third-party supply is a powerful process. It requires substantial preliminary work, as it is the cornerstone of world-class procurement.

CPO Insights from Chris

Building the momentum around strong spend management is linked to how successful you can be in the execution of the sourcing process. As you launch categories of spend, the key is to identify areas in which you have a strong executive sponsor who is willing to lead from the front. Team formation is critical: Procurement should be seen as the facilitator of the process; the team should be cross-business and cross-functional with regional input where applicable. On occasion, the sponsor of the team will be different from the executive sponsor. Sometimes, this is the best scenario because executives do not always want to be engaged with some of the week-to-week challenges that inevitably occur.

I have failed in the past by not putting the correct team together or establishing alignment with the proper active sponsor. Setting up the best team and the right sponsor guarantees successful implementation, once an agreed-upon strategy is in place. If you employ a fact-based decision-making process during the strategy- development phase, you can overcome the range of change-management challenges that will arise during implementation.

When you are launching category teams, the fewer the better. Pick the critical few categories that can deliver strong value and execute successfully with minimal change. This will build trust with the stakeholder community. The cornerstone of success is linked to the categories you pursue.

6 Cross-functional Team Leadership

Topic Area Assessment Statements

Review these statements from your perspective as a procurement leader. If you "strongly agree" with all of the statements, you may wish to skip to the next topic. But, if you have some doubts about any of them, we recommend that you read this chapter and engage in some self-reflection.

- Procurement team leaders know and consistently use excellent team-leadership tools and techniques.
- Procurement team leaders document category teamwork efforts to ensure ease of team-member assimilation.
- Important teams within my sphere of control regularly and consistently assess their performance and continue to improve.

Topic Introduction: Cross-Functional Team Leadership

There are numerous books (at least 221 on Amazon now!) on cross-functional team leadership, and some are well worth reading.[1] What is important, however, is that the sourcing and supplier-management processes are team sports (i.e., for the teams to be successful, non-procurement people must participate as members). As it should be, Procurement is typically the team leader's "day job." It is the leader who must put in place effective team processes that make efficient use of team members' time and attention; if the meetings are poorly run and waste time, nobody will attend. Properly executed, these processes will build trust and create a procurement value proposition at individual and functional levels and continue to evolve.

Topic-Specific Nomenclature

As in most industries, procurement professionals use a range of terminology with specific definitions. The following terms and definitions are used in this section:

- ***Sponsor***: A senior leader, almost always a stakeholder outside Procurement (yet inside the company) with a vested interest in the outcome of a project; often, the senior budget-holder.

1. Kelsey, Dee and Plumb, Pam. *Great Meetings! Great Results*. Portland, Maine, Hanson Park Press, Inc., 2004, is an excellent resource.

Cross-Functional Team Leadership Tools

The following tools, which are used with every cross-functional team, create a simple framework that helps develop effective team processes and reassure stakeholders that their time will be not be wasted.

Team Tool
Team Charter Every team must have a team charter that outlines: • Team objectives (typically in A/RQSCI terms) • Team members • Team sponsor • Sub-category(ies) included, excluded, or held for later consideration The charter is drafted during the team-launch process; any team-requested changes must be reviewed and approved by the same body that established the team.

<table>
<tr><th colspan="2">Team Charter</th></tr>
<tr><td>Category Name and Purpose:
• Category-Name________________________
• Develop and implement a worldwide category strategy that satisfies the corporate business requirements

Category Boundaries:
• All business units worldwide

Category Sponsor Responsibilities:
• Work with team to set goals and expectations.
• Be the team champion to the organization.
• Remove roadblocks.
• Monitor and approve team progress.</td>
<td>Category Manager and Responsibilities:
• Category Manager________________________
• Facilitate creation of team charter and team.
• Understand customer business requirements.
• Determine with sponsor and Procurement Leadership Team (PLT) input, the scope of the project.
• Lead team in establishing clear goals and objectives.
• Facilitate team understanding of current process for the category.
• Develop strategic-source plan that meets current and future business needs.
• Lead short-term and long-term procurement strategies to accomplish objectives.
• Maintain appropriate records.
• Establish and publish key milestones through project management.
• Demonstrate leadership skills when working with team.
• Ensure completion and implementation of source plan.

Team Members: Procurement, Sales, Distribution, Manufacturing
Extended Support-Team Members: Legal, IT, Marketing</td></tr>
<tr><td>Category Sponsor Expectations (i.e., targets, constraints, budgets):
• Responsibilities:
– Agree to support team objectives
– Monitor team performance
– Provide guidance
• 50 percent of leaders' and 25 percent of team members' time committed to project
• Team to develop project budget for approval within two weeks of first meeting
• Strategy complete within sixteen weeks of kickoff meeting
• Monthly progress report required by third business day of month</td>
<td>Team Member Responsibilities:
• Participate in refining team charter, scope, and objectives.
• Participate in the source planning and business-case processes.
• Provide support to phase in source plan.
• Attend all assigned meetings.
• Assist in data gathering and information development.
• Represent Procurement and the business at large.
• Solicit input from stakeholders regarding business needs.
• Extended support team member responsibilities.
• Provide support in specific areas of expertise.

Facilitator and Responsibilities:
• Facilitator Name________________________
• Work with team leader to plan all meetings.
• Keep team on process.
• Capture and document meeting and conference call output.</td></tr>
</table>

4P Agenda

Typical agendas include the topic to be covered and the time allocated. This is helpful but not nearly enough information to produce an effective meeting. The 4P agenda adds

Purpose: Why is the topic being covered? Why is this an important use of team time? Summarize the desired outcome for the topic. Discussion, decision, and review of information are typical examples.

Process: This is a detailed review of:

- How will the topic be covered? Options include discussion, presentation, data sharing, among others.
- Who will lead the topic? What are the expectations of the other participants?
- Is there any pre-work? If so, what are the applicable templates so that the work is consistent among members?

Preparation: What pre-work must be completed in advance of the meeting? Typical examples include reading materials, subteam meetings, and presentation development. Be explicit about the details required and who must do the work.

Payoff: What is the team now positioned to accomplish after the topic is covered? Examples include decisions made, consensus developed, and understanding of nuances.

Note: If either the purpose or payoff is unclear, the topic may not belong on the agenda, or it may need to be reframed.

4P Agenda					
Topic	**Purpose**	**Process**	**Preparation**	**Payoff**	**Timing**

Note: Thanks to Noelle Lee for her recommendation to add the fourth "P" – Preparation. This addition aids clarity tremendously.

Team Tool
Meeting Minutes
Meeting minutes are required for every meeting of consequence. *Do not hold the meeting if minutes will not be taken.*
The format is easiest to use if it mirrors the 4P agenda. Follow the topic flow, and add the respective decisions (from the decision log) and next steps/responsibilities (from the action plan).

Meeting Minutes		
Topic	**Decisions**	**Next Steps/Responsibilities**

Action Plan
The action plan documents follow-up tasks, responsible party, and due date for completion.
Note: Action plans typically are built during the flow of the conversation, which can result in a large number of tasks, often disproportionately weighted toward a few key team members. At the close of a meeting, it is a good practice to review the tasks for clarity and the ability of the team members to realistically accomplish all of their commitments. If necessary, rebalance the responsibilities, and make it clear that the due dates are real.

Action Plan		
Task	**Responsible Party**	**Due Date**

Decision Log
The goal of the decision log is to turn casual or implied agreements into conscious commitments. Each team will decide which decisions are important enough to document on the decision log. Once they are documented, these decisions should be considered to be mandates, unless they are changed by the team with the sponsor's concurrence. Appropriate use of decision logs builds transparency and trust among team members.

Decision Log		
Decision	**Rationale**	**Date Decided**

Team Tool
"Parking Lot" (aka "Car Park" in Europe) Parking lots are used in team meetings to manage topics that are interesting but not on the agenda—what we call '"rabbit holes." When a conversation veers off topic, it is called a "rabbit hole." The proper way to handle a rabbit hole is to assign it to the parking lot, if everyone agrees. Once it has been "moved," the discussion of the appropriate agenda topic can resume. At the close of the meeting, it is important to review the topics moved to the parking lot to determine whether they should be: • Addressed at a future meeting • Addressed individually • Ignored • Covered at a different meeting *Note: Always formally close the parking lot at the end of the meeting. Failure to do so will result in the team refusing to use the parking lot in the future, because it will view it as a way to "blow off" topics.*

Parking Lot ("Car Park")	
Topic	**Resolution at the end of the meeting**

Team Process Check-In

During the life of a cross-functional team, it is often helpful to do a formal "check-in" with the team members to determine whether the process is working for them. We use a simple survey format as described below. Best practice is for the submission of input to a neutral, trusted third-party (this can be HR or an external consultant) for compilation of the results. The results are best reviewed with the team leader privately so that he or she is positioned to positively and non-defensively address any team concerns during the subsequent team-wide review.

Check-in Structure

Three groupings of assessment statements:

- Overall team-related questions to include quantitative scoring
- Fellow team-member questions to include quantitative scoring
- Open-ended, qualitative questions, which are high-level commentary on the team dynamics

Our team...	**Our fellow team members...**
1. Is on track to achieve the assigned goals	1. Work cooperatively on team assignments
2. Is very productive	2. Listen to the ideas of others with open minds
3. Explores all potential options	3. Constructively criticize ideas, not people
4. Values everyone's contributions	4. Resolve conflicts constructively
5. Demonstrates comfort with other team members	5. Avoid disruptive side conversations
6. Stays on track/topic during meetings	6. Allow everyone to participate; do not dominate discussions
7. Plans ahead	7. Are succinct and avoid long anecdotes and examples
8. Comes together easily	8. Respect those who are not present
9. Shares the same goals	9. Ask questions when they are confused
10. Contributes to discussions	10. Are responsible for the team's success
11. Has developed ways to resolve conflict and reach consensus	11. Discuss with and offer ideas to the team
12. Attends all team meetings and sticks to the agenda	12. Are aware of other team members' feelings
13. Is prepared for meetings	13. Consistently go above and beyond to help others
14. Understands the team's expectations	

Check-in Qualitative Open-ended Questions:

1. The top three areas that are working well for this team are ...
2. The top three areas that are not working as well at this time are ...
3. My hope for this team is ...
4. My fear for this team is ...
5. Any open comments or teammates worthy of recognition (and why)

Team Process Check-In

The team facilitator/coach summarizes the findings and reports the aggregate results (quantitative and qualitative) to the entire team. The resulting team conversation on next steps to address any key findings is typically a watershed event for the team and leads to increased team effectiveness and member satisfaction.

Summary

Procurement teams are almost exclusively future-oriented. This creates a positive environment for the team. It is up to the team leader to maintain this outlook. Proper use of the team tools helps guarantee success.

CPO Insights from Chris

There is nothing more frustrating than a poorly structured meeting with no clear agenda, time management, action plans, or follow-up. We all attend such meetings, but they can be avoided. This first step is adequate preparation: having proper pre-work in place, circulated, and reviewed in advance by all attendees, including the meeting chair. This step alone demonstrates respect for everyone's time and input, encourages constructive debate, and allows tracking and follow-up of action plans and decisions. Even when decisions are made, we often find ourselves revisiting them at the next meeting. The root cause is usually that the decision was not clearly documented and agreed upon in a collaborative way. The team tools we have shared in this chapter are extremely powerful, especially when running cross-functional teams. Use of these tools promotes the professionalism and discipline we sometimes lack in running a business.

TEMPLATE: Team Charter

Category Name and Purpose:

Name of the category/sub-category
Purpose/use of the product or service

Example:

- Hotels – North America
- Transient rooms near company facilities

Category Boundaries:

Which sub-categories are included?
Which sub-categories that could be included are expressly excluded?

Example:

- Includes transient rooms in NYC, LA, Atlanta, and Des Moines
- Does not include long-term stays or group meetings and events

Team Leader and Responsibilities:

Name and title of team leader (procurement professional)

Example:

- Billy Bob Jones, Global Travel category manager
- Facilitate team through the strategic-sourcing process including strategy development, approval, and implementation
- Manage sponsor and procurement stakeholders

Category Sponsor and Responsibilities:

Name and title of the sponsor
Agreed sponsor responsibilities

Example:

- Mary Smith, VP Corporate HR
- Identify cross-functional team members, and secure their time to participate on the team.
- Ensure access to company data – historical and projected.
- Monitor team progress, and address issues as needed.
- Support strategy implementation.

Team Members:

Names, titles, and locations of team members

Example:

- Mario Jimenez, sales manager, Los Angeles
- Theresa Hanson, partner, Human Resources, Des Moines
- Sergio Albanez, production leader, Atlanta
- Wanda Smith, Corporate Human Resources, NYC

Category Sponsor Expectations:

Includes targets, constraints, budgets, and the like:

Example:

- Create a strategy no later than ___________ (set date)
- Develop a compelling implementation plan with key stakeholder support
- Up to $XXXX available for team meetings and related out-of-pocket expenses

Team Member Responsibilities:

Tasks and expectations for the team members

Example:

- Participate in team activities—expected at 25 percent of time through implementation
- Support team process and decisions
- Represent stakeholder and business needs
- Complete assigned tasks

TEMPLATE: 4P Agenda

Meeting Title, Date, Venue					
Topic	**Purpose**	**Process**	**Preparation**	**Payoff**	**Timing**
A short phrase summarizing the topic	*Why the group is covering the topic*	*How the topic will be covered and who is responsible*	*Who needs to do what to ensure the topic is successfully addressed*	*What the group is ready to do after completing the topic*	*Estimated running time for the topic*
Example: Introductions and Agenda Review	To know who is in the room, what we plan to accomplish, and how the meeting will run	Meeting leader (named person) to introduce himself/herself and then all participants to do so in turn Meeting leader to review the agenda and all participants to ask any clarifying questions	Meeting leader to draft and distribute the agenda in advance All participants to read the agenda, note areas of responsibility, and prepare for the meeting	All participants know who is attending and understand the meeting flow; last-minute suggestions are addressed	15 minutes

TEMPLATE: Meeting Minutes

Meeting Title, Date, Venue					
Topic	**Resolution**	**Decision(s)**	**Follow-up Actions**	**Responsible Party**	**Timing**
A short phrase summarizing the topic	*A summary of the discussion (Note: not a transcript; omit confidential details)*	*Any core decisions (as captured on the decision log in the meeting)*	*What needs to be done after the meeting as a result of the discussion*	*Who (named) is responsible for the follow-up actions*	*The deadline for completing the follow-up actions*
Example: Develop Business Requirements	Team reviewed, edited, and assigned tentative weightings to the draft business requirements.	Additional stakeholder input is needed; survey the key stakeholders from the stakeholder map.	Develop a survey, and send to the identified stakeholders.	Team leader (named person) and two team members (their names).	Within two weeks of the meeting, the survey is sent with responses due two weeks after that.

7 Business Requirements Analysis

Topic Area Assessment Statements

Review these statements from your perspective as a procurement leader. If you "strongly agree" with all of the statements, you may wish to skip to the next topic. But, if you have some doubts about any of them, we recommend that you read this chapter and engage in some self-reflection.

Business requirements—detailed value requirements—are established for every category of spend within your span of responsibility:

- Stakeholders and Procurement collaboratively establish business requirements.
- The process of developing business requirements has generated trust and rapport between Procurement and stakeholders.
- Category business requirements distinguish between wants and needs.
- Category business requirements support current and future business strategies.
- Category business requirements are **S**pecific, **M**easurable, **A**ction-oriented, **R**ealistic, and **T**ime-bound (SMART).

Topic Introduction: Business Requirements Analysis

Analysis of business requirements is the foundation for rational procurement activities. It underpins all sourcing and supplier-management activities, from strategy creation, through supplier analysis, to performance management of the selected suppliers. In short, use of business requirements to develop a strategy is part of what separates professional sourcing from uninformed shopping. All procurement practitioners should understand and consistently practice the development of business requirements.

Business requirements, as the hallmarks of the organization, are dynamic. Every category of spend shows continued evolution of business requirements; the only difference is the rate of change.

A Couple of Hints

Too many procurement organizations believe they know the business requirements and do not need to discuss them with stakeholders before developing a strategy or approaching suppliers. This is a fatal mistake that will waste tremendous amounts of goodwill, trust, and time. Don't do it. The development of business requirements is a cross-functional activity!

Topic-Specific Nomenclature

As in most industries, procurement professionals use a range of terminology with specific definitions. The following terms and definitions are used in this section:

- ***Criteria*** – Differentiating elements used to make a decision. In the case of procurement-related product-and-service-selection decisions, these criteria will relate to Availability, Regulatory Approval/Ethical Right to Use, Quality, Service, Cost, and Innovation. (A/RQSCI)
- ***Go/No Go versus Scalable*** – Go/No Go criteria are "must haves." These are the nonnegotiable aspects of the decision. Often (but not always), these are related to ethical and regulatory requirements. Scalable requirements are desirable as in "would like to have." These are the criteria that, when all of the Go/No Go criteria are satisfied, will sway the decision between otherwise equal providers.
- ***Weighting*** – The relative importance of the scalable criteria to the specific audience. This is most often a stakeholder-based decision. We highly recommend that stakeholders start with a total of one hundred possible points for all scalable criteria and apportion points according to their business priorities (i.e., if cost is most important, then it should receive the most points).

Related Context

It all began with Abraham Maslow.[1]

Abraham Maslow

While all business requirements are different and the rates of change vary, there is a better practice for identifying and segregating them, regardless of the source. This practice is modeled on the premise of the hierarchy of needs posited by Abraham Maslow.

Maslow wrote that the most basic needs—physiological and safety—must be met before "higher-order" needs become relevant.

In short, a person who is homeless or in fear for his life is unlikely to worry too much about his self-esteem or Facebook status!

1. Source for picture and Hierarchy Diagram is Wikipedia; Abraham Maslow.

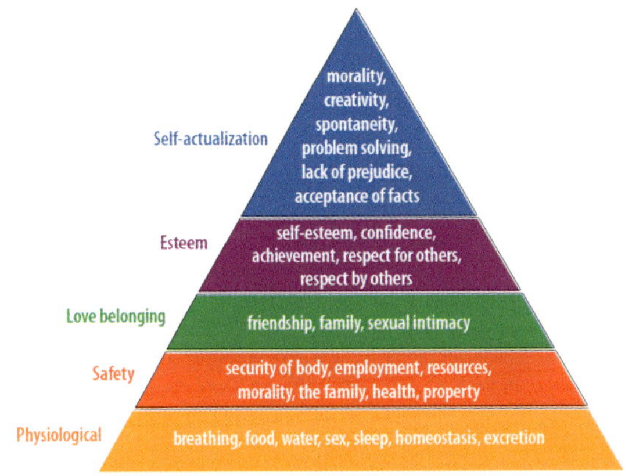

An individual, however, who is very secure in his or her basic needs and is pursuing self-actualization, will revert to the lowest unmet need in a crisis. The pursuit of an advanced degree becomes irrelevant in the face of a life-threatening disaster.

How is this related to procurement and business requirements?

The Tool: Business Requirements Analysis

Business requirements follow a similar pattern of evolution. Once the basics are met, the more esoteric requirements are worthy of consideration.

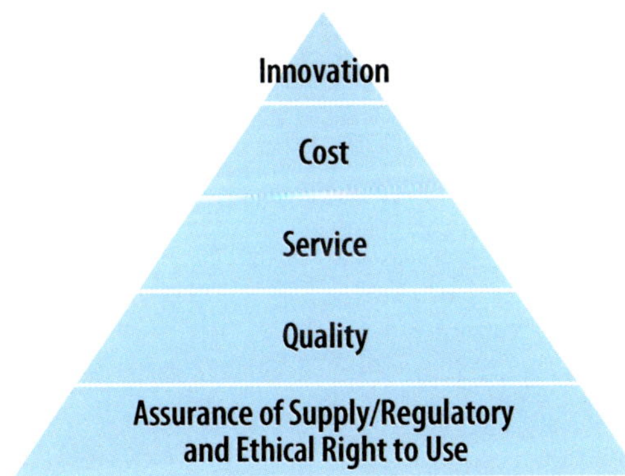

The model of business requirements that we recommend from most basic to highest order is:

- Assurance of Supply/Regulatory and Ethical Right to Use
- Quality
- Service
- Cost
- Innovation

Additionally, some business requirements are absolutely mandatory; if the mandatory requirement is missing, the remaining requirements are irrelevant. These are the "must" or "Go/No Go" requirements. Using fact-based decision making, other parameters are of variable value, depending on the category, and are "wants" or "scalable" requirements.[2] The following is a discussion of each of the business requirements.

2. The process of determining business requirements and sorting between "Go/No Go" and weighting is derived from Criteria-Based Decision Making described in *The New Rational Manager - An updated edition for the new world.* 2013 by Charles H. Kepner, and Benjamin B. Tregoe. This is an excellent reference for all sourcing professionals.

Innovation

Innovation is typically the highest-order business requirement. All other requirements must be met before innovation is even considered.

Notable exceptions occur when:

- Differentiable product opportunities arise (i.e., first to market with a sustainable advantage)
- Potential for life-saving products or services exists

In these circumstances, the status of innovation will rightly move to the fore as the most important business requirement. Innovation is typically a scalable (not a Go/No Go) criterion.

Cost

Cost is typically a high-order business requirement, meaning that it is not relevant to stakeholders until or unless all other more basic requirements are met. *Note: Cost does not equal price; cost is the total cost in use.*

Procurement is almost always focused on controlling cost and generating savings. This is fine—it is part of Procurement's mission—but it is irrelevant and harmful if the fundamental supply is compromised. Cost can be either scalable (e.g., less is better) or a Go/No Go (e.g., a not-to-exceed budget).

Service

Service is related to the delivery of the goods or services and the ongoing support.

Service can be either scalable (e.g., more is better) or a Go/No Go (e.g., a minimum amount required).

Quality relates to the functional specifications—the performance of the product or service in use.

Quality

Quality can be either scalable (e.g., fewer defects per million) or a Go/No Go (e.g., a defined size/speed with fixed variations specified).

Assurance of Supply/Regulatory and Ethical Right to Use

Assurance of Supply and Regulatory/Ethical Right to Use is the most rapidly evolving business requirement.

Assurance of Supply is focused on the ability to obtain adequate supply at the consuming locations. Assurance of Supply is typically considered a Go/No Go (e.g., the North American factories are kept in supply), but it often has a scalable component (e.g., can supply North America and Europe, which is potentially scaled higher; the supplier can supply more locations in addition to the mandatory Go/No Go location).

Regulatory/Ethical Right to Use embraces the entire spectrum of regulatory approval, corporate social responsibility, and the broader topic of compliance. This is a rapidly expanding area with widespread supply-chain and end-customer marketing implications. It is typically considered a Go/No Go (i.e., the FDA approves the supply; there are no child-labor suppliers), but it often has a scalable component (i.e., the supplier is approved by all relevant regulatory agencies and can supply globally, or the supplier is proactively working with Tier 2 suppliers to address working conditions).

The development of business requirements is best accomplished by a cross-functional team as follows:

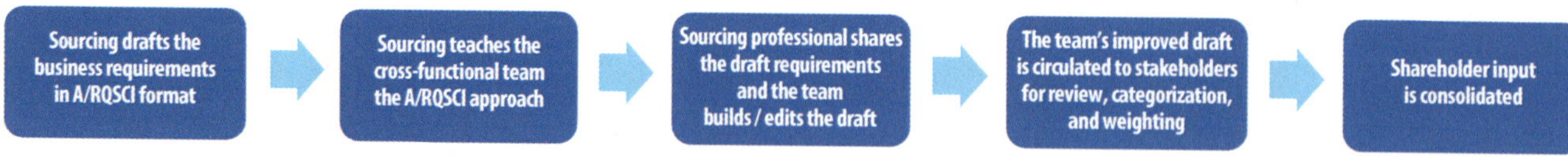

Business Requirements Development Process

Business Requirements Development Step	Comments
The sourcing professional independently drafts the business requirements in the A/RQSCI format.	The sourcing professional must possess market knowledge in order to be credible with the team. This sets the stage for the team to demonstrate awareness of the current requirements and the applicable category nomenclature.
The sourcing professional teaches the team the A/RQSCI business requirements construct.	As the representative of the procurement organization, the sourcing professional is the leader of the process. He/she must teach the tool to others when necessary. We recommend that the leader demonstrate the tool to provide a comprehensive view of the A/RQSCI requirements and stress that this is not a cost-driven exercise.
The sourcing professional presents draft business requirements to the team, and the team edits as needed to ensure clarity and consistency with actual current needs and anticipated future needs.	The team must be able to fully edit the requirements, which cannot be presented as "final." The team must then determine whether the requirements fully comply with the SMART acronym: **S**pecific, **M**easurable, **A**ction-oriented, **R**ealistic, and **T**ime-bound. Initially, most business requirements are vague statements (e.g., "Good quality") and emerge, after much discussion, with clearer definitions. This refining of the business requirements is a vital part of the process and continues as long as the category is actively managed.
Edited business requirements are distributed to key stakeholders for additional edits and weighting (i.e., Go/No Go or, if scalable, the relative weight).	Key stakeholders must be involved in the business-requirements definition and weighting process if they are expected to value and accept the resulting strategy. Business requirements are key to the process; without them, this is merely mindless shopping. Engage the stakeholders in the manner that is most likely to build engagement. For some, this will be an internal survey; for others, it will be face-to-face interviews.
Consolidate all stakeholder input, and finalize business requirements and weightings.	All input must be considered. In too many cases, the input from small businesses or geographies is ignored in favor of the dominant businesses and geographies. If this choice to ignore the input from small businesses and geographies is made, the charter must be expressly modified to limit the category-strategy efforts accordingly. It is not acceptable to collect business requirements, ignore the input that is not consistent with the predominant geography/business, and then try to impose a solution on the areas whose input was ignored. This may sound obvious, but it often happens in global organizations.

Sample Business Requirements *

Office Supplies (Global) Example		
Parameter	**Business Requirements (as developed by the team and then reviewed, categorized, and weighted by stakeholders)**	**Categorization / weighting**
A	• Wide choice and range of products requested by the company available (i.e., more than 30,000 SKUs) • Range of products available in the language required by the local laws and the requisitioners	***Go/No Go***
R	• Compliance with necessary regulations (i.e., paper/pulp laws) • Code of conduct acceptance (ethical purchasing policy)	***Go/No Go***
Q	• Products suited for purpose described in catalogue • Generic options available in range of products • Sustainable "green" options available in range of products	***20%***
S	• Scale: Ability to scale on geographic coverage of the company sites, which also allows for home-based sales associates to leverage company-negotiated prices (i.e., > company's one-hundred-plus locations worldwide) • Delivery: >Ninety percent of core item deliveries can be made most efficiently, reasonably (per each country's market requirement), and cost effectively, with desktop deliveries as an option • Account Management: Centralized with strong reporting; quarterly performance review against Key Performance Indicators (KPIs); invoice quality is ≥ 99 percent accurate; customer-service response rate of ≤24 hours; local management and service at each company site • Process: 24/7 online catalogues, supplier's website, and EDI capabilities available at all locations where the company can implement this; simplified where possible	***30%***
C	• Competitive pricing • No unapproved price increases • Can demonstrate continuous cost-education program (i.e., demand management, shipping cost, substitutes of an equal or lower cost, effective purchasing)	***40%***
I	• Inclusion of supplier diversity requirements (for US)	***10%***

** Felicia Cheng, an outstanding sourcing professional, in concert with her cross-functional team, developed the above.*

Summary

Developing high-quality, actionable business requirements is some of the hardest work a cross-functional team will do. It is also among its most important work, having an impact well into the future. This is not a "one-and-done" process; it is continually refined as the needs of the business evolve over time. Do not rush the process. As stakeholder trust is built, the protective wall of "wants" will come down. The results of this step are used to set the strategy, select suppliers, create contracts, and manage ongoing performance.

CPO Insights from Chris

Whether you are looking at a category of spend or ways to run the function, business requirements should be/must be integral to the decision-making process. As you look at a category of spend, be sure that you are clear on the criteria to determine a strategy. Executing a strategy that does not meet the clear needs of the business is suicidal and a job-limiting move. SMART criteria that will drive the selection process are an important part of the dialogue one must have with the stakeholder community. Have a clear understanding of needs versus wants in the decision-making process. There is a tendency to mix wants and needs; seek to understand and educate stakeholders on the difference. A "need," such as a paper pad to write notes, versus a "want," a leather-bound pad with my name embossed on it, can drive up cost and be seen as unnecessary waste.

Cost is not the primary driver for the stakeholder community. Stakeholders expect Procurement to pursue the entire range of business requirements. Stakeholders are, however, very interested in solutions that lead to improved total cost of ownership (TCO). Ethics must be front and center in Procurement's decision-making criteria, as it is the cornerstone of trust with our stakeholder community. Procurement's reputation can suffer if our behavior and reward systems are too focused on price. The full range of business requirements must be measured and rewarded.

TEMPLATE: Business Requirements, page 1

Your Name:	Sub-category:
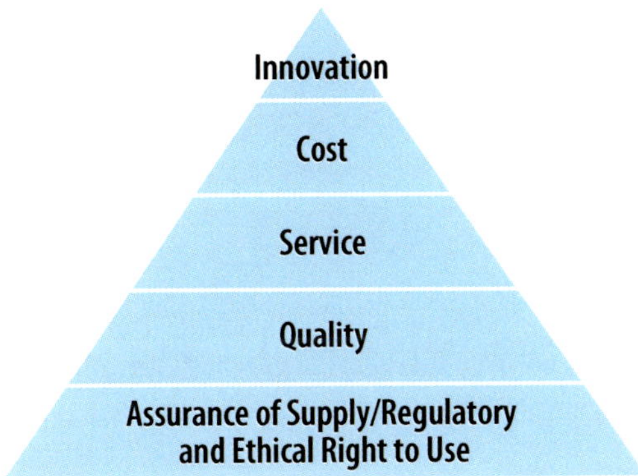 	**Business requirements include:** • Assurance of Supply/Regulatory and Ethical Right to Use • Quality • Service • Cost • Innovation Options include "Go/No Go" and "scalable"; scalable must be weighted; all criteria must be SMART.

Business Requirement	**Draft Requirement**	**Go / No Go or Scalable** If scalable, estimate weighting
Assurance of Supply/ Regulatory and Ethical Right to Use		
Quality		
Service		
Cost		
Innovation		

TEMPLATE: Business Requirements, page 2

Your Name:	Sub-category:

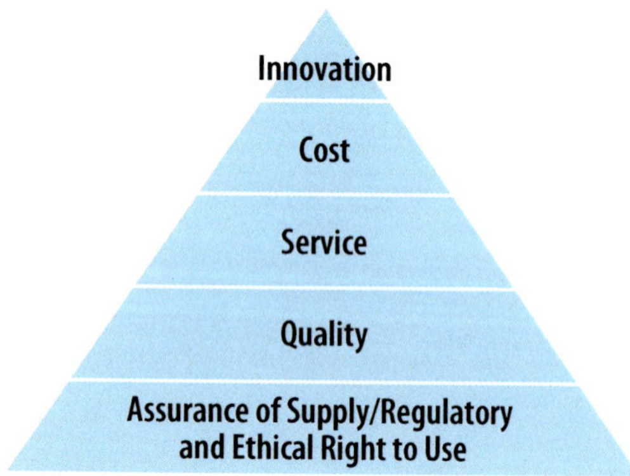

Business requirements include:

- Assurance of Supply/Regulatory and Ethical Right to Use
- Quality
- Service
- Cost
- Innovation

Options include "Go/No Go" and "scalable"; scalable must be weighted; all criteria must be SMART.

Business Requirement	Draft Requirement	Associated KPI
Assurance of Supply/ Regulatory and Ethical Right to Use		
Quality		
Service		
Cost		
Innovation		

8 Layered Strategy Development

Topic Area Assessment Statements

Review these statements from your perspective as a procurement leader. If you "strongly agree" with all of the statements, you may wish to skip to the next topic. But, if you have some doubts about any of them, we recommend that you read this chapter and engage in some self-reflection.

- Category strategies evolve over time to reflect the changing needs of the business.
- Category strategies evolve over time to reflect the ability of the business to effect change.
- Category strategies evolve over time to reflect increasing stakeholder trust and confidence in procurement.

Topic Introduction: Layered Strategy Development

Our experience confirms that there is a typical progression of potential category strategies that reflects:

1. The evolving needs of the business over time (e.g., changing business requirements)
2. The business leadership's growing ability to effect change, which enhances its confidence in the procurement function to effectively use third-party solutions

The creation of "layered strategies" is one of the most important and fundamental activities of the procurement function. Layered strategies permit full realization of the procurement value proposition beyond price by enabling sales growth while supporting bottom-line contributions.

The most simplistic view of typical layered strategies is below:

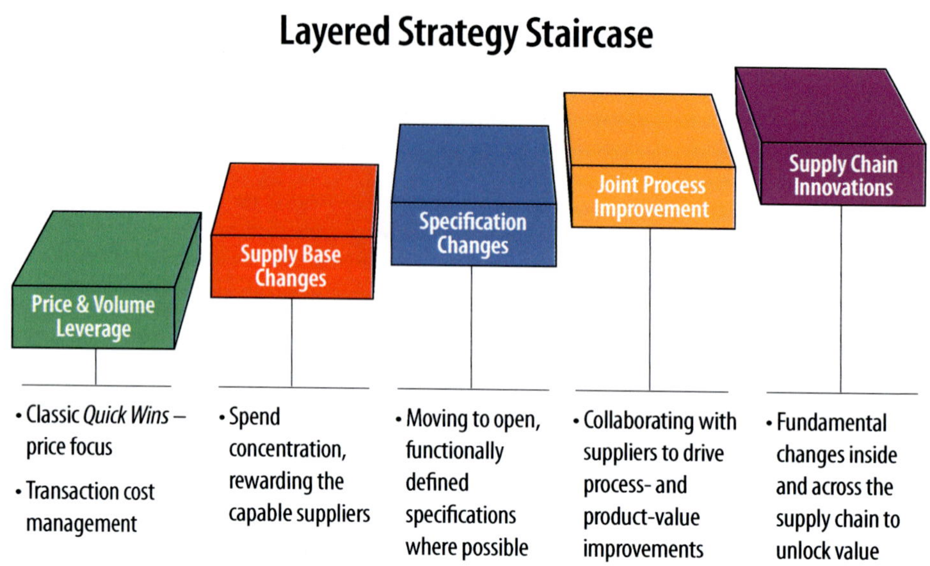

Not every category will include every step; some categories may skip steps. What these steps embody, however, are increased commercial capability (inside the company and with associated suppliers) and elevated trust in the procurement function.

Cross-functional teams, through a comprehensive strategic-sourcing process, are best at developing layered strategies. Procurement departments occasionally believe themselves capable of developing strategies in a vacuum and then "selling" those strategies to stakeholders. This is a flawed approach and misses the invaluable buy-in that occurs during joint strategy development. Procurement departments generally do not have line accountability for the resources to enable a change across the company.

Topic-Specific Nomenclature

As in most industries, procurement professionals use a range of terminology with specific definitions. The following terms and definitions are used in this section:

- ***None.***

The Tool: Layered Strategy Development

Step 1 – Price and Volume Leverage

Procurement Activities:

- Assess price and term variability from the same supplier through global spend analysis.
- Negotiate with current suppliers (standardize the best terms provided globally or true market-based terms if original terms were disconnected from current market practice).
- Maximize cash for the company.
- Automate transactions if applicable.
- Revise contracts (beware of extending terms and compromising strategic options).
- Communicate results to stakeholders.
- Explore hedging options.

Procurement Competencies Required:

- Spend analysis
- Negotiation
- Communication
- Financial acumen

Stakeholder Activities:

- Understand communications and support procurement efforts to improve basic terms.

Supplier Activities:

- Respond to procurement requests, such as request for Interest/ Proposal/Quotation (RFI/P/Q).
- Negotiate in good faith.
- Avoid the temptation to play stakeholders against Procurement for short-term gains.

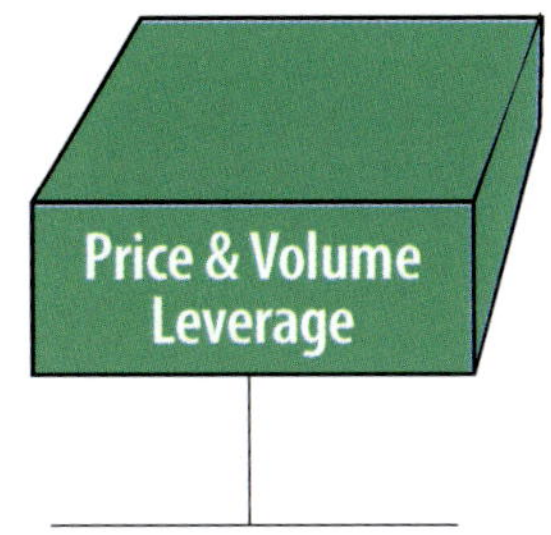

- Classic *Quick Wins* – price focus
- Transaction cost management

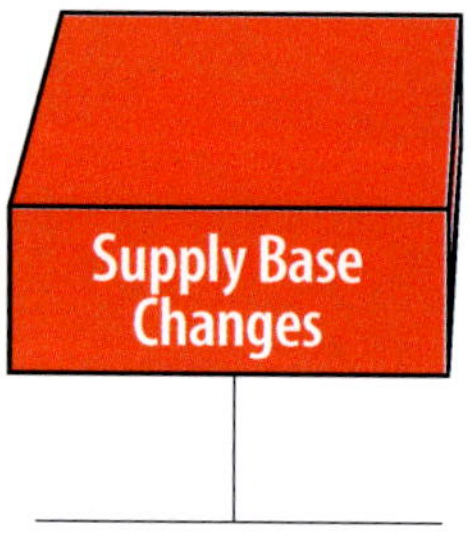

• Spend concentration, rewarding the capable suppliers

Step 2 – Supply Base Changes

Procurement Activities:

- Leverage the capability of the current supply base, and move volume to reflect supplier interest (e.g., better terms).
- Negotiate with current suppliers, rewarding "better suppliers."
- Revise contracts (beware of extending terms and compromising strategic options).
- Conduct supplier forums if consistent with the category strategy and broader business priorities.
- Communicate results to stakeholders.

Procurement Competencies Required:

- Detailed business-requirements analysis
- Supplier performance measurement
- Negotiation
- Change- and project-management skills
- Communication – written and verbal; multiformat

Stakeholder Activities:

- Participate in the development of comprehensive business requirements.
- Participate fully in supplier-measurement activities.
- Understand communications; support procurement efforts to improve delivery and move business within the current supplier community.

Supplier Activities:

- Respond to procurement requests – RFI/P/Q.
- Negotiate in good faith.
- Avoid the temptation to play stakeholders against Procurement for short-term gains.

Step 3 – Specification Changes

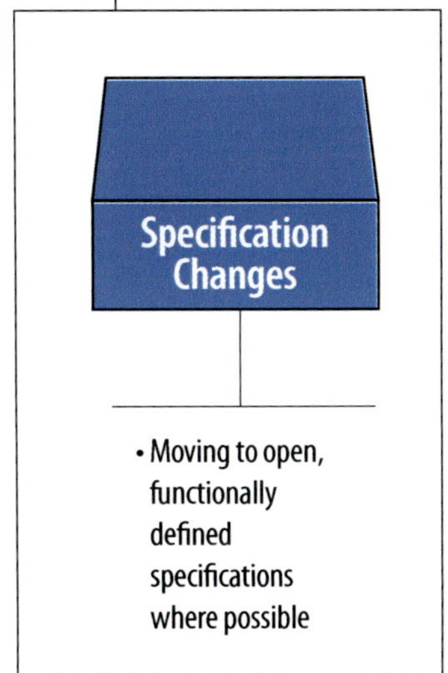

Procurement Activities:

- Change the incoming specifications to more closely align with market specifications, where possible and where this will not compromise the value proposition of the end product (e.g., moving away from company-specific requirements that unnecessarily restrict choice).
- Negotiate with current and potential suppliers.
- Revise contracts (beware of extending terms and compromising strategic options).
- Communicate results to stakeholders.

Procurement Competencies Required:

- Market intelligence
- Negotiation
- Change- and project-management skills
- Communication – written and verbal; multiformat.

Stakeholder Activities:

- Understand specification requirements at a functional level to enable changes that remove supplier-specific nuances and brands, while protecting the efficacy of the selected supply.
- Participate in all communications to demonstrate "a united front" to the suppliers.

Supplier Activities:

- Respond to procurement requests – RFI/P/Q.
- Participate in hiring and firing processes in good faith.

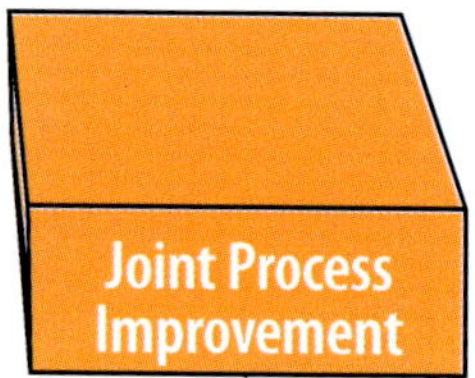

- Collaborating with suppliers to drive process- and product-value improvements

Step 4 – Joint Process Improvement

Procurement Activities:

- Establish joint company-supplier team(s) to develop product and process innovations.
- Establish contractual agreement(s) to protect new intellectual property; be sure that protections are fair and reflect the relative risks and investments.
- Negotiate for complete, holistic relationship with suppliers and affected stakeholder communities.
- Continuously measure performance.
- Revise contracts when necessary to protect intellectual property (process- and product-based).
- Communicate results to stakeholders.

Procurement Competencies Required:

- Joint team creation and facilitation
- Change-management skills
- Complex contracting, including intellectual-property provisions
- Complex negotiation, including team-based scenarios with stakeholders
- Communication – written and verbal; multiformat.

Stakeholder Activities:

- Participate as an equal partner with Procurement to establish joint teams.
- Participate in the negotiations.
- Implement targeted value engineering.

Supplier Activities:

- Enable buyer competitive advantages in the market through differentiated product and service capabilities.
- Negotiate in good faith.

Step 5 – Supply Chain Innovations

- Fundamental changes inside and across the supply chain to unlock value

Procurement Activities:

- Identify opportunities for outsourcing/insourcing or joint ventures that will create clear competitive advantages for the buying organization and/or ensure focus on core competencies.
- Document processes (if outsourcing).
- Establish joint governance (in all scenarios).
- Establish contractual agreements to protect new intellectual property; ensure that protections are fair and reflect the relative risks and investments.
- Negotiate for a complete, holistic relationship with the supplier and affected stakeholders.
- Conduct ongoing performance measurements.
- Revise contracts as necessary.
- Communicate results to stakeholders.

Procurement Competencies Required:

- Documentation of the process, including change-management enablers
- Complex, joint-governance establishment and leadership
- Complex contracting, including intellectual-property provisions
- Complex negotiation, including team-based scenarios with stakeholders
- Communication – written and verbal; multiformat. *Note: Communications at this level are complex and highly nuanced. These efforts are invariably team-based with communication experts participating fully.*

Stakeholder Activities:

- Participate as an equal partner with Procurement to establish joint teams.
- Participate in negotiations.

Supplier Activities:

- Enable buyer competitive advantages in the market through differentiated product and service capabilities.
- Negotiate in good faith.

Summary

The core purpose of Procurement's sourcing/category-management elements is to develop insightful layered strategies. Deep collaboration and trust—the hallmarks of a valued procurement function—are the result of including stakeholders in the development and implementation processes.

This approach is deceptively simple, yet extremely powerful. Category segmentation, followed by the development of associated layered strategies, permits a clear focus on developing procurement competence and organizational planning. An organization with a preponderance of categories that are managed at the lower-strategy levels is likely to include category outsourcing as one of its strategic options. Categories that are managed at the highest levels, on the other hand, will require very skilled procurement professionals who possess the full gamut of technical and change-leadership skills. Understanding this mix is the key to achieving world-class procurement delivery, while maintaining the lowest possible costs.

CPO Insights from Chris

The key to achieving success in leveraging the "Layered Strategy Staircase" is linked to the maturity of the procurement function within the company and Procurement employees' ability to deliver a layered approach to the categories they lead. The staircase can be used as a tool to determine how Procurement can deploy its resources and where to place them to support the organization efficiently and effectively. The staircase highlights where investment is needed to secure significant value. As part of a dialogue with senior executives, the staircase helps clarify the value proposition.

When you start the journey to bring professional sourcing to a company, you must earn the trust of the stakeholder community. Typical procurement transformation will start at the bottom of the staircase; price-and-volume leverage is typically 80 percent of the delivery. The implementation process is comparatively easy with minimal disruption to the company. Ideally, the stakeholders are delighted with the results and ready to embrace more advanced strategies.

Proposing advanced strategies can be a double-edged sword if the stakeholder community sees the role of Procurement solely at the lower end of the staircase. If you maintain this approach, it is extremely hard to change the mindset without engaging in a true category-management approach. To successfully create a real partnership between Procurement and the company, map out a layered strategy that progressively builds trust and confidence in Procurement.

Procurement team members must be able to lead cross-functional teams through the strategy-development process. This typically involves a virtual team; the interpersonal dynamics and meeting management are complex, yet essential. The higher the discussion moves up the strategy staircase, the higher the degree of change necessary to obtain the benefits. You will need strong stakeholder buy-in to be truly effective.

9 Category Spend-Governance Mapping

Topic Area Assessment Statements

Review these statements from your perspective as a procurement leader. If you "strongly agree" with all of the statements, you may wish to skip to the next topic. But, if you have some doubts about any of them, we recommend that you read this chapter and engage in some self-reflection.

- Procurement and stakeholders collaboratively define and agree on the current category spend-governance decision rights and responsibilities (i.e., who is authorized to make each aspect of the sourcing/supply decisions).
- Procurement and stakeholders collaboratively define and agree to the future category spend-governance rights.
- Procurement and stakeholders collaboratively define and resource the appropriate change-management activities to achieve the desired future state category-spend governance decision rights and responsibilities.

Topic Introduction: Category Spend-Governance Mapping

An in-depth understanding of current Procurement and stakeholder beliefs and perceptions around the third-party decision-making process is crucial for effective procurement. Specifically, who believes that they are responsible for selecting vendors and are empowered by the company to do so? Who approves the associated terms and conditions? Who is expressly authorized by the business to perform these tasks? Does behavior match company authorization? Are those who are making the decisions actually authorized to do so? These fundamental questions are very revealing and must be fully understood by all procurement members and the relevant stakeholders.

Topic-Specific Nomenclature

As in most industries, procurement professionals use a range of terminology with specific definitions. The following terms and definitions are used in this section:

- ***Spend-governance mapping*** – Identifying all of the elements of a spend decision and which parties believe they play a role at each stage.
- ***Decision-rights analysis*** – The analysis of who is authorized to make the decision in question. Often, multiple parties believe that they are authorized to make a decision; yet, the true budgetary and fiduciary responsibility lies with a much narrower subset (sometimes, one person) of those who believe they are empowered.

The Tool: The Category Spend-Governance Mapping Process

The description below is at a category level but can and should be done at any level in the organization.

1. Select a category/sub-category that enables you to focus with clarity (e.g., "laptops" are more specific and can be analyzed more readily than "all other IT hardware," which is vague and has many diverse stakeholders).
2. Establish the parameters of the sourcing process that apply in this case (e.g., design specifications, licensing, supplier selection, supplier qualifications, commercial negotiations, ongoing supplier management, etc.).
3. Identify who meets these criteria, and describe their respective roles in objective terms, such as who (which person, team member, stakeholder) decides, recommends, reviews/approves, or observes.
4. Using your professional experience and judgment, identify areas for improvement, the benefits of making those improvements (or the costs of inaction), and the steps you recommend.
5. Incorporate an "as-is" chart for the work of the sourcing team from communication and change-management perspectives. Then, create a "should-be" chart for the future. Take the necessary steps to align the team's current implementation strategy with the future chart.

Select a Category Spend-Governance Mapping Model

The two commonly applied methods are RACI and RAPID (defined below). RACI is the most commonly used method, but the distinction between responsible and accountable will confuse some people. RACI is primarily intended for establishing work-performance roles and responsibilities, and RAPID is used to describe the discrete elements of decision making; these topics frequently intersect. Our advice is to use the model that produces clarity for the participants. Do not force-fit either model if it is not advancing participants' understanding.

RACI stands for:	RAPID stands for:
• **R** = Responsible – the person who owns the problem or project • **A** = to whom R is accountable – the person who must sign or approve the work before it is acceptable • **C** = should be consulted – the person who has information and/or capability necessary to complete the work • **I** = should be informed – the person who must be notified of progress and results, but need not be consulted	• **R** = Recommend – This person initiates or drives the process. The R is the "go-to" person who sticks with the process from start to finish, makes certain that others understand what they need to do, and keeps things moving along. In other words, the R does most of the work to secure the decision by advocating for his/her recommendation and addressing concerns and objections. • **A** = Agree or approve – This person must "agree with" or "approve" a decision. An A has a vote and a veto. Naming someone as an A means that the organization needs that person's support. Generally, the more people with an A who must agree with or approve a decision, the more time and effort it takes to make that decision. Not every decision requires an A. The A level is often the executive-management team or the board of directors. • **P** = Perform – This person carries out the decision once it has been made. • **I** = Input – This person must be consulted before a decision is made. Although an I has the right to be heard, he/she does not have a vote or a veto. Including someone as an I means that the organization values that person's opinion. • **D** = Decide – This person has the official authority to make the decision. At the outset of almost all category-strategy efforts, there are several people who believe they own elements of or all of D. Your change-management efforts include clarifying and confirming these decision rights and, occasionally, moving them to a new person or organization. RAPID is a service mark of Bain & Company, Inc.

Summary

Understanding the "as-is" category governance map is a prerequisite to making changes. The mapping process identifies the current participants and the roles they believe they play in the sourcing- and supplier-management processes. As Procurement's value proposition evolves, the category-spend governance typically changes; Procurement moves from a performer of tactical buying to a participant in strategic decision making. When you plan this process, be sure to include proactive, comprehensive change-management activities.

CPO Insights from Chris

Procurement leaders must deliver services and programs aligned with stakeholder expectations. Sometimes, these are low-level, tactical expectations; other times, they are high-level, strategic expectations. Each of these, however, requires very different procurement skill sets and strategic orientations.

We often underestimate the need to put in place the right governance structures and sensing mechanisms. The road map will vary by company and can build on existing mechanisms, such as operating committees or business teams. Standalone procurement councils and regional councils help manage the overall governance. The recommendation is clear: Establish a structure and include business, regional, and other functional associates.

TEMPLATE: Category Spend-Governance Mapping

Category: ______________________________

Sub-category: ______________________________

Item: ______________________________

As-is Governance				Should-be Governance	
Sourcing parameter (all that apply)	**Participant and role** (name, title, function)	**Reasoning behind role**		**Participant and role** (name, title, function)	**Reasoning behind role**
Design			To be completed by the cross-functional team as part of strategy development; likely to vary based on both the selected strategy and how strategy evolves		
Specify components or service elements					
In-license					
Supplier inclusion/ consideration					
Supplier qualification					
Supplier selection					
Strategy development					
Strategy selection					
Commercial negotiation					
Supplier management					

10 Lean Portfolio

Topic Area Assessment Statements

Review these statements from your perspective as a procurement leader. If you "strongly agree" with all of the statements, you may wish to skip to the next topic. But, if you have some doubts about any of them, we recommend that you read this chapter and engage in some self-reflection.

- Category analysis clarifies how our company is approaching key supply markets.
- Category analysis includes an objective view of supply-market dynamics.
- Category analysis overlays our current organizational behaviors and how they affect the company's standing in the supply markets.
- Category strategies seek to maximize the company's value in their respective markets.

Topic Introduction: Lean Portfolio

The Purchasing Portfolio Analysis, originally developed by Peter Kraljic in the early 1980s, is the benchmark analysis tool used in nearly every procurement organization.[1] Many firms modify it slightly to fit their needs, but the essence remains the same: understanding the fundamentals of supply markets and how the buying organization is linked to these markets. This is an incredibly powerful tool and invaluable for developing strategic insights.

In its original form, Kraljic's Purchasing Portfolio Analysis was a two-by-two matrix.

Profit Impact	High	**Leverage**	**Strategic**
	Low	**Non-Critical**	**Bottleneck**
Portfolio Analysis		Low	High
		Supply Risk	

1. Peter Kraljic, "Purchasing Must Become Supply Management," *Harvard Business Review*, September 1983.

This tool served procurement professionals and stakeholders well for years and enabled meaningful distinctions and strategic insights. In Erik Stavrand's consulting practice, however, I noticed the following important phenomena around this tool:

1. The strategic choices between "strategic" and "leverage" are stark, and many practitioners avoided the line (or the areas near the lines) and missed meaningful options and value.
2. The tool does not take into consideration the very real changes in production techniques as a result of Lean/Six Sigma production techniques and the subsequent impact on supply relationships.
3. The axes are a source of near-constant consternation and "tinkering" by procurement practitioners and their companies.

I developed the "Lean Portfolio" model as a variant of the Kraljic approach (with full deference to the elegance of Kraljic's model) to address these phenomena. Lean Portfolio is one of the trilogy tools that must be used in every category: Category Segmentation, Lean Portfolio, and Customer Segmentation.[2]

Topic-Specific Nomenclature

As in most industries, procurement professionals use a range of terminology with specific definitions. The following terms and definitions are used in this section:

- ***None.***

2. Jonathan O'Brien, Category Management in Purchasing: A Strategic Approach to Maximize Business Profitability, Kogan Page, 2012, pp. 140-152. Jonathan refers to this tool as 'Portfolio / Kraljic Analysis' and is completely faithful to Peter Kraljic's model and approach. This is one of the few areas where Jonathan and I use different approaches.

The Tool: Lean Portfolio

The fundamental approach is by means of the two-by-two matrix with an additional quadrant.

Market Difficulty/ Supply Risk			
	High	**Critical** *In the original Kraljic model*	**Strategic** *In the original Kraljic model*
	Moderate		**Lean** *NEW to the Lean Portfolio model*
	Low	**Acquisition** *In the original Kraljic model*	**Leverage** *In the original Kraljic model*
Lean Portfolio		Low	High
		Profit/Spend Impact	

The axes on this tool are straightforward and very similar to the original Kraljic model.

X-Axis–Profit/Spend Impact: The most helpful way to think about this axis is *the degree to which practitioners can affect spend or profit if they apply their best professional efforts.* In some categories, great effort will result in substantial value; in other categories, the best possible work results are negligible to nonexistent.

Y-Axis–Market Difficulty/Supply Risk: This is a straightforward axis and readily understood by most practitioners.

Market Difficulty includes:

- **Supply choices** –Can your needs be met by multiple suppliers (at least two of whom behave competitively), or are they restricted to a single supplier? *Note: Sole sources of supply are inherently more difficult than multiple supply scenarios with vastly more risk of disruption.*

- **Category complexity** –Is the category complex, with changing specifications, or stable, as with a basic commodity?

Risk includes:

- **Market Competitiveness** –Is the market open and competitive, or are oligopolies (i.e., control of a commodity or service in a given market by a small number of companies or suppliers), cartels, or monopolies at work?

Lean Portfolio with the key business requirements overlay

An overlay of the core business requirements by category makes the inherent distinctions between the quadrants more apparent and actionable.

<table>
<tr><td rowspan="3">Market Difficulty / Supply Risk</td><td>High</td><td>Critical
Primary business requirement
• Assurance of supply</td><td>Strategic
Primary business requirement
• Innovation (new, differentiated products or services) with the potential to create enduring competitive advantage</td></tr>
<tr><td>Moderate</td><td rowspan="2">Acquisition
Primary business requirement
• Cost (in use) minimization</td><td>Lean
Primary business requirement
• Innovation (process-focused) with potential to create production advantages (services and products); reducing total cost through end-to-end process improvements</td></tr>
<tr><td>Low</td><td>Leverage
Primary business requirement
• Reducing cost (total cost) to market parity (all basic requirements are assumed to be met and equal)</td></tr>
<tr><td colspan="2" rowspan="2">Lean Portfolio</td><td>Low</td><td>High</td></tr>
<tr><td colspan="2">Profit/Spend Impact</td></tr>
</table>

Note: The core, basic business requirements of quality (fitness for purpose), service, and regulatory/ethical right to use must be met in all quadrants.

Lean Portfolio with common category overlay

Common categories regardless of industry are slotted below.

Market Difficulty / Supply Risk		Profit/Spend Impact: Low	Profit/Spend Impact: High
	High	**Critical** • Branded products (when written into the buyer's specifications) • Niche chemicals, orphan drugs	**Strategic** • New product-development services (e.g., university research for pharma) • Brand strategy and creative
	Moderate		**Lean** • Primary packaging • Outsourced services
	Low	**Acquisition** • Lawn services • Local catering	**Leverage** • Bulk chemicals • Temporary labor
Lean Portfolio		Low	High
		Profit/Spend Impact	

Lean Portfolio can also provide insights into the different staffing requirements for the distinct sections of the chart.

Lean Portfolio with appropriate Procurement staffing personality/approach overlay

The adjectives and descriptors highlight the most appropriate procurement approach in each quadrant.

<table>
<tr><td rowspan="3">**Market Difficulty / Supply Risk**</td><td>High</td><td>**Critical**
Procurement Approach
• **Technical expert**–When supply is limited by the underlying specifications, it is very helpful to enlist an expert who can lead the process to "unlock" the specification.</td><td>**Strategic**
Procurement Approach
• **Diplomat**–The goal is to create value that is mutually beneficial. This is almost always a senior-level endeavor and requires a clear vision and finesse in dealing with conflict.</td></tr>
<tr><td>Moderate</td><td rowspan="2">**Acquisition**
Procurement Approach
• **Automation/e-catalogs/ trainee**–The goal is to reduce transaction costs. A trainee can learn in these categories, if required, with little risk.</td><td>**Lean**
Procurement Approach
• **Process/Value Engineering Expert**–
Joint process improvement activities are the goal, and expertise leading these efforts is required.</td></tr>
<tr><td>Low</td><td>**Leverage**
Procurement Approach
• **Aggressive**–This quadrant requires the exercise of appropriate, ethical power to ensure that market credibility is maintained. Indeed, if power is not exercised in leverage, it is lost in all categories.</td></tr>
<tr><td colspan="2" rowspan="2">**Lean Portfolio**</td><td>Low</td><td>High</td></tr>
<tr><td colspan="2">**Profit/Spend Impact**</td></tr>
</table>

As in all strategic-analysis tools, one of the objectives of using Lean Portfolio is to examine where the company is now (based on current company behaviors) and whether the category strategy should be to stay where it is currently positioned or to move to another quadrant. The next steps will depend on the overall layered strategy. Alternatives include staying in the quadrant or seeking to change the way suppliers perceive the buying organization and moving from one quadrant to another.

Current quadrant	Key Business Requirement	***Stay*** **in the current quadrant and how to stay**	***Move*** **to a different quadrant (which one) and how to move**
Acquisition	***Cost (in use)*** – minimization	• Automate processes with e-catalogs and full electronic data interchange (EDI). • Deploy P-cards (i.e., company-issued credit cards).	**Leverage** 1. Aggregate spend of similar, low-value categories, such as: — Pens and paper become office supplies. — Catering and security become facility services. — Air and hotel become travel. 2. Manage aggressively for value.
Leverage	Reducing ***Cost (Total Cost)*** to market parity	• Stay connected to the market with electronic requests for information, proposals, and quotes (eRFx). • Periodically move business within the supply base and to new suppliers. Market credibility is vital. In too many firms, an annual eRFx exercise results in no supply changes. This practice reduces credibility. We are NOT advocating changing all of the suppliers all the time. Rather, it is important to make selected, high-visibility changes.	**Lean** • To access supplier-provided process improvements **Acquisition/Leverage Blend** • Disaggregate spend when the business requirements evolve to provide focus on the core, high-value needs. An example is moving low-use chemicals to a distributor in acquisition and moving to a direct relationship with the manufacturer on the remaining bulk chemical(s).
Lean	• ***Innovation*** (process-focused) with potential to create production advantages (services and products) • Reducing ***Total Cost*** through end-to-end process improvements	• Be sure that process improvements deliver promised value through rigorous management of joint improvement teams. • Extend the length of the relationship. • Establish comprehensive metrics with targets for improvement. • Maintain market surveillance.	**Leverage** • Reconnect with the market when new providers offer better/more services or when underlying business requirements change. **Strategic** • Jointly create new products or services (rare but possible); establish a joint venture.
Strategic	• ***Innovation*** (new, differentiated products or services) with the potential to create enduring competitive advantages	• Joint new product/service creation teams • Joint ventures • Open-book financials • A focus on true win-win, where the standard is, "what is good for one party is equally good for the other party" • Extended relationships • Market surveillance	**Lean/Leverage** • Reconnect with the market when new providers offer better/more services or when the underlying business requirements change.
Critical	• ***Assurance of supply***	Assure supply continuity through heightened surveillance of: • Supplier strategy (Are they discontinuing production/supply?) • Supplier financials • Other supply-chain risks • Market surveillance for new market entrants	**Leverage** • Change the specifications to "unlock" the restrictions and connect with the market. **Strategic/Lean** • Change the specifications as in Leverage, and launch joint-value creation activities. • *Note: This is possible but, in our experience, extremely unlikely due to the behavior dynamics that typically emerge when the buying organization is "locked" in the Critical quadrant by the selling organization.*

All Roads Lead to Leverage

For years, we advocated strategies that began with the typical starting behavior of the company in the Critical quadrant, either actually locked into supplier specifications or behaving as such with inordinately long supply agreements (e.g., five years firm; fixed for corrugate). The objective market view places most categories in the Leverage quadrant. In short, the vast majority of categories start the strategy-development process with artificially constrained choices when, in actuality, they exist in markets with wide choices.

It is a simple and liberating fact that most categories and markets are objectively in the Leverage quadrant. This is a beautiful thing for the sourcing professional!

The question we often hear is about moving *directly* from Critical to Strategic/Lean (i.e., *How can I move from a position where I have no choice, little or no market power, and a supplier who is exploiting this situation to a position of high mutual trust and joint-value creation?*). Reread that sentence. Do you think it is likely that this person could move directly from Critical to Strategic/Lean? It *is* possible but, in more than twenty years in the field, we have never seen it done successfully. It is vital to exercise all of the benefits of Leverage (with both suppliers and stakeholders) before committing to a higher-level relationship. We use the analogy of "dating relationships" to drive this point home.

Quadrant	Dating/Nature of the Relationship Analogy
Acquisition	Internet chat rooms/"speed dating"
Leverage	Uncommitted dating
Lean	Committed dating/engaged
Strategic	Marriage (best explained as two parties who are jointly creating a new future that neither could create individually)
Critical	"Shotgun wedding," where one party is disadvantaged relative to the other; the balance of power/interest is not equal.

Is it possible to move from a "shotgun wedding" to an ideal marriage? While it may be possible, it is very, very unlikely.

This analogy helps most practitioners understand the difficulty of moving from "Critical" directly to "Strategic"; mutual trust and respect must be created before Strategic is possible. It is best to get a "divorce" from the Critical relationship, move to Leverage, reconnect with the market, and then consider the other options.

Summary

Lean Portfolio is a "must-use" tool for every category. It requires full participation by the affected stakeholders. As such, it is included in most stakeholder-education sessions due to its broad applicability to business strategy. Stakeholders understand and really appreciate the insights gained from using the Lean Portfolio tool. They come to see procurement professionals in a new light (i.e., as strategic thinkers) and are then willing to invest time and resources to move categories out of the Critical arena (or quadrant).

CPO Insights from Chris

Lean Portfolio is a great business tool that we sometimes fail to use when we engage with our internal stakeholders and external supply partners. The way we behave as individuals or as a company when it comes to category-specific behaviors and strategies determines how effective we are at maximizing the value in the supplier/customer relationship.

The first step in applying Lean Portfolio is to educate and train the internal stakeholder community around how we are behaving versus how we should be behaving. Over the years, I have found that we often think we are behaving one way when, in fact, we are exhibiting completely opposite behaviors. If we use a packaging category, such as corrugated boxes, the desired behavior is Leverage (many suppliers and generic specifications), which would push us to a bid cycle or auction in terms of tactics. The supplier will try to move us to a Critical position based on printing or tightness of specifications; however, it pays to remember that there are plenty of suppliers.

The operations staff will consider factors such as site values, as well as supplier proximity, the length of the relationship, or the additional value that a supplier is providing. If you step back and reflect, the tasks are to determine how to move from the current behavior to the new behavior and to identify the opportunity associated with driving the change.

Changing stakeholder perceptions about categories requires an investment of time and effort—our personal capital. As we evaluate a category with the portfolio tool, we can gauge how much personal capital to invest in changing the way we manage the category. We may recognize, as sourcing professionals, that some categories are objectively in Leverage; but stakeholders may, as longtime consumers in a specialized area, believe that the category is Critical. This is a common occurrence. We must, however, address these stakeholder misperceptions to build our relationships with them. These perceptions were not established overnight, and it may take years to correct them.

Lean Portfolio is a core tool that, when used correctly, will help you obtain buy-in from stakeholders in effecting change within the organization. It is one that all procurement leaders must become familiar with and use.

TEMPLATE: Strategic Analysis – Lean Portfolio

<table>
<tr><td colspan="4">Your Name:</td><td>Sub-category:</td></tr>
<tr><td rowspan="3">Market Difficulty/ Supply Risk</td><td>High</td><td rowspan="2">Critical</td><td>Strategic</td><td rowspan="5">X-Axis – Profit/Spend Impact – the degree to which practitioners can affect spend or profit if they apply their best professional efforts.
Y-Axis – Market Difficulty/Supply Risk
Market Difficulty includes:
• Supply choices
• Category complexity

Risk includes:
• Market competitiveness</td></tr>
<tr><td>Moderate</td><td rowspan="2">Lean</td></tr>
<tr><td>Low</td><td>Acquisition</td></tr>
<tr><td colspan="2" rowspan="2">Lean Portfolio</td><td>Low</td><td>Leverage
High</td></tr>
<tr><td colspan="2">Profit/Spend Impact</td></tr>
</table>

Current company behavior description and corresponding quadrant (as in C-above, the user will plot the C)	
Objective market view of the sub-category (as in O-above, the user will plot the O)	
Strategic Insights	
Who needs to know these insights?	
• Inside Procurement	
• Outside Procurement	
How will you share the insights?	
Names	**Methods & Core Messages**

11 Category Segmentation

Topic Area Assessment Statements

Review these statements from your perspective as a procurement leader. If you "strongly agree" with all of the statements, you may wish to skip to the next topic. But, if you have some doubts about any of them, we recommend that you read this chapter and engage in some self-reflection.

- My team and I understand the fundamental drivers for each category.
- My team and I understand the price-determination approaches for each category, which are consistent with the underlying drivers.
- My team and I deploy advanced tools, such as cost modeling and supply and value-chain analysis, when warranted.

Topic Introduction: Category Segmentation

The truth is simple: Not all categories are the same; there are fundamental differences between categories, and understanding these differences is critical to developing a successful strategy.

The core parameters for every category are:

1. Specifications – Who "owns" or establishes the specifications?
2. Pricing – How is pricing established, and who controls the process?
3. Intellectual property – Who "owns" the intellectual property?

Analysis of these parameters yields tremendous insights. Category segmentation is one of the "trilogy tools" – Category Segmentation, Lean Portfolio, and Customer Segmentation – that must be used in every category.[1]

Topic-Specific Nomenclature

As in most industries, procurement professionals use a range of terminology with specific definitions. The following terms and definitions are used in this section:

1. Jonathan O'Brien, *Category Management in Purchasing: A Strategic Approach to Maximize Business Profitability,* Kogan Page, 2012, pp. 80-85. Our approaches are otherwise largely consistent.

- ***Fundamental category drivers*** – These include the core elements of setting specifications and ownership of intellectual property.
- ***Intellectual property*** – The common definition includes brands, trademarks, service marks, patents, unique know-how, trade secrets, and proprietary working methods.

The Tool: Category Segmentation

The fundamental approach is the two-by-two matrix.

Number of Sellers with Access to the Intellectual Property	More than one (>1)	**Tailored**	**Generic**
	One	**Custom**	**Proprietary**
Category Segmentation		One	More than one (>1)
		Number of Customers	

First, the axes are different from those customarily used.

X-Axis – Number of Customers: How many willing and ready customers are there for this exact category—from a single customer to more than one. Some refer to this as "multiple" or "many," but it is enough to just have two to fundamentally change a category. It is not necessary to have many.

Y-Axis – Number of Suppliers *with Access to the Intellectual Property:* This is often labeled with only the number of suppliers. The resulting analysis is flawed, as it must also address intellectual-property ownership. Intellectual property, whether in the form of a copyright, patent, design, idea, or brand, is what sets the suppliers apart in this analysis. Again, the range is from one to more than one.

Category Segmentation Differentiating Parameter Overlay

If we overlay the fundamental parameters, the inherent distinctions between the quadrants become apparent and useful.

Number of Sellers with Access to the Intellectual Property	Number of Sellers		
	More than one (>1)	**Tailored** • Specifications – owned/set by the buyer • Pricing – cost to produce (see Note 1 below) • Intellectual property – owned by the buyer	**Generic** • Specifications – owned/set by the market • Pricing – market price • Intellectual property – owned/set by the market
	One	**Custom** • Specifications – jointly owned by the buyer and seller (functional specification is set by the buyer; design specification is set by seller) • Pricing – target price (see Note 2 below) • Intellectual property – typically owned by the seller (see Note 3 below)	**Proprietary** • Specifications – owned/set by the seller • Pricing – value (to the user; highest possible use) • Intellectual property – owned/set by the seller
Category Segmentation		One	More than one (>1)
		Number of Customers	

Notes:

1. *Although the pricing model in the "Tailored" quadrant is the cost to produce, few sellers will start with this approach. Most sellers start with value pricing if they can (this is a rational way to maximize profit). If value pricing is the long-standing approach between the seller and the buyer, the change dynamic will take time. Do not give up!*

2. *In order to be effective, target pricing must involve a design competition. Absent such a competition, target pricing is likely to revert to a budget price, and the incremental value will be lost.*

3. *Ongoing ownership of intellectual property is a fundamental goal of most strategies. It is possible for a buyer to secure a breakthrough design (Custom quadrant) and then move ongoing production to preferential production conditions (Tailored quadrant).*

Category Segmentation: Common Categories by Quadrant

The following shows commonly occurring categories across the tool.

Number of Sellers with Access to the Intellectual Property			
	More than one (>1)	**Tailored** • Contract manufacturing • Call centers • Imprinted items – typical company-branded sales giveaways	**Generic** • Bulk chemicals • Basic commodities
	One	**Custom** • High-end creative design, engineering, architecture, flavors (see Note 1 below) • "Made for an individual consumer" items or services	**Proprietary** • Branded items/services/performers • Patented items
Category Segmentation		One	More than one (>1)
		Number of Customers	

Note 1: The Custom quadrant and "high-end" creative agencies (marketing) confuses many practitioners. In the example of architects, there are hundreds of thousands of architects. Each architect, however, will create a unique solution to meet the buyer's request. Consider the Freedom Tower in New York City. When the call went out for design submissions to replace the World Trade Center towers a number of firms submitted competing designs (design specifications) to meet the functional specifications set by the buyer. The designs were reviewed and ultimately the design by Daniel Libeskind was selected.

Typical strategic and business requirements priorities for each quadrant (see page 103)

Note 2: The fundamental business requirements must always be delivered: assurance of supply, compliance with regulatory and ethical right to use, quality conformance, and adequate service.

One of the side benefits of category segmentation is that it helps determine which further analyses, such as cost modeling and supply and value chain, are appropriate and which are unnecessary.

Quadrant	Parameters	Typical Categories	Discussion
Generic	• **Specifications** – owned/set by the market • **Pricing** – market price • **Intellectual Property** – owned/set by the market	• Bulk chemicals • Basic commodities	• The focus of business requirements is typically on cost (see Total Cost versus Price). • *This is the most appropriate quadrant for e-auctions and similar marketplace tools.* • Cost modeling is not typically warranted unless there is a suspicion of a "false market" (e.g., "Pharma alcohol" instead of Alcohol USP. It happens!).
Tailored	• **Specifications** – owned/set by the buyer • **Pricing** – cost to produce • **Intellectual Property** – owned by the buyer	• Contract manufacturing • Call centers • Imprinted items (typical sales giveaways)	• The focus of business requirements is competitive costs (pricing should be "cost to produce" or "open book" with full transparency). The primary focus is typically on service. • *This is an appropriate quadrant for e-auctions. The auction may address service parameters.* • Cost modeling is expected for all categories in Tailored at an absolute level; percentage allocations of cost are not sufficient (i.e., must use real numbers, not just "plug" numbers that add up to 100 percent).
Proprietary	• **Specifications** – owned/set by the seller • **Pricing** – value (to the user; highest possible use) • **Intellectual Property** – owned/set by the seller	• Branded items/ services/ performers • Patented items	• The focus of business requirements is assurance of supply. The buyer is purchasing in this quadrant as a result of the specifications; somehow, stakeholders are reducing the potential supply market to 1. Even if there is an opportunity to change and "unlock" the specification, this should be the goal. • *This is NOT an appropriate quadrant for e-auctions.* • Cost modeling is not useful for Proprietary categories.
Custom	• **Specifications** – jointly owned by the buyer and seller (functional specification is set by the buyer; design specification is set by seller) • **Pricing** – target price • **Intellectual Property** – typically owned by the seller (see discussion)	• "High-end" design, engineering, architecture, flavors • "Bespoke" items	• The focus of business requirements is innovation—securing new ideas/capabilities that will drive competitive advantage. • *This is NOT an appropriate quadrant for e-auctions.* • Cost modeling is useful for establishing a range of "should costs" upon which to base the floor for target pricing. • The path to success in Custom is based on doing the following: 1. Clearly determine the functional specifications. 2. Determine the most innovative suppliers in the category (if necessary, break out the design/innovative elements of the category from the production elements. Once the design is set, tailored producers can produce it). 3. Conduct a supplier briefing. 4. Conduct a design competition. This is mandatory! 5. Select the appropriate winner based on your requirements. 6. Contract for ownership of the intellectual property—both design and production rights—to enable portability.

Category segmentation is used to drive strategic insights, in addition to the prior insights. It is an incredibly powerful tool.

Additional insights:

1. Buyers are *typically* strongest in Generic and Tailored quadrants; sellers are strongest in Proprietary and Custom quadrants. Business requirements drive the appropriate quadrant. *Note: The differences between buyers' and sellers' markets are profound, and the relative strength of the buyer/seller relationships can reverse, with the seller becoming strongest in a capacity-constrained, high-demand generic market. In a seller's market, the seller can become very strong in Generic and Tailored (e.g., when oil spikes at $150/barrel, oil service providers are in demand as the "oil-services and production industry" seeks to rapidly capitalize on the market change; when oil later falls to $50/barrel, the buyer/supplier power dynamic reverses).*
2. The goal of marketing is to create nuances, real and perceived, that lead to product differentiation. This is a nice way of pulling buyers from the Tailored and Generic into Proprietary and Custom quadrants. Buyer beware!
3. Bundled goods and services invariably contain products and services from multiple quadrants. These are then priced at the value they deliver to the buyer. This means that a relatively high price will probably include generic goods and services at a "bundled price." The recommendation is simple: Always open or break the bundle to determine if the aggregate value is appropriate.
4. Technology is affecting categories in new and different ways. Printing is historically a Tailored category; large, lithograph-type printing is still Tailored. Small-batch, digital printing, however, is more appropriately considered Generic. This is great for the buyer and reflects the power of competitive markets and supply-chain innovation.
5. Additional pricing methods exist outside the four included in category segmentation. Of most concern to the buyer is budget pricing. This almost always disproportionately benefits the seller, as the pricing is set by an artificial constraint disconnected from the fundamentals of the product/service and the category. This is particularly an issue in the capital and construction categories where a "use-it-or-lose-it" budgeting approach is common. We strongly encourage stakeholders *not* to share budget information with suppliers.

Summary

Category segmentation is a must-use tool for every category. As such, it is included in most stakeholder-education sessions due to broad applicability to business strategy; stakeholders understand and really appreciate the insights from this tool. Stakeholders will see Procurement in a new light (i.e., as strategic thinkers) and are then willing to invest time and resources to move categories out of the Proprietary/Custom quadrants.

CPO Insights from Chris

Category segmentation builds on the strategic thinking begun in Lean Portfolio. It is important to correctly identify whether the category is Generic, Tailored, Custom, or Proprietary as you prepare to deploy limited resources. Short-term gains typically come from Generic and Tailored categories, which are simpler and can be staffed by the less-skilled associates, whereas Proprietary and Custom require associates with higher skills.

Resource deployment is impacted or driven by category segmentation; look for subject-matter expertise in the Custom or Proprietary categories. Driving incremental value requires procurement associates to use different skill sets to engage the stakeholder community. Similar to Lean Portfolio analysis, it is also important to compare current and desired future behavior—the essence of a category strategy.

TEMPLATE: Category Segmentation

Your Name:	Sub-category:

Number of Sellers with Access to the Intellectual Property			
More than one (>1)	**Tailored**	**Generic**
One	**Custom**	**Proprietary**
Category Segmentation	One	More than one (>1)
	Number of Customers	

X-Axis – Number of customers: How many willing and ready customers are there for this exact category from one (a single customer) to more than one.

Y-Axis – Number of suppliers with access to the intellectual property: Intellectual property, whether a design, idea, or brand or protected by copyright, patent, or registration, is what sets the suppliers apart in this analysis.

Current company behavior description and corresponding quadrant (as in C-above, the user will plot the C)	
Objective market view of the sub-category (as in O-above, the user will plot the O)	
Strategic Insights	
Who needs to understand and appreciate these insights?	
• Inside Procurement	
• Outside Procurement	
How will you share the insights?	
Names	**Methods & Core Messages**

12 Customer Segmentation

Topic Area Assessment Statements

Review these statements from your perspective as a procurement leader. If you "strongly agree" with all of the statements, you may wish to skip to the next topic. But, if you have some doubts about any of them, we recommend that you read this chapter and engage in some self-reflection.

- Category strategies analysis reveal the way suppliers are behaving toward the company.
- Category analysis infers how suppliers perceive the company's value, based on their behaviors.
- The company is maximizing its relative value in the marketplace.
- My team and I factor apparent supplier behaviors/perceptions of the company into negotiation and supplier-value management plans.

Topic Introduction: Customer Segmentation

As with categories, not all customers are the same or equal in value. Sales organizations, like procurement organizations, are measured by their performance. Keys to success are the ability to produce results with limited resources and prioritize efforts. We rarely know how important we are to our suppliers, but it is often possible to infer our ranking based on observing their behavior and attitudes. The assessment of this ranking is an important lens to apply as you develop strategic insights.

Customer segmentation is one of the trilogy tools—Category Segmentation, Lean Portfolio, and Customer Segmentation—that must be used in every category:[1]

Topic Specific Nomenclature

As in most industries, procurement professionals use a range of terminology with specific definitions. The following terms and definitions are used in this section:

- ***None.***

1. Jonathan O'Brien, *Category Management in Purchasing: A Strategic Approach to Maximize Business Profitability,* Kogan Page, 2012, pp. 153-157. Jonathan refers to this tool as *"Supplier Preferencing" (i.e., To whom do suppliers prefer to sell and why?).* Our approaches are otherwise largely consistent.

The Tool: Customer Segmentation

Attractiveness of the Account			
	High	**Investment**	**Key**
	Low	**Automated**	**Maintenance**
Customer Segmentation		Low	High
		Value / Profitability of the Account	

Y-Axis – Attractiveness of the Account

- Growth potential – Is the account growing, shrinking, or flat?
- Difficulty to work with – Are there multiple approval levels in different countries for every issue, or is approval straightforward and responsive?
- Payment predictability – Does the account pay on time or dispute/delay every payment? What are the payment terms?

X-Axis – Value/Profitability of the Account

How much is the account worth—a small amount with infrequent sales or a large amount with high profits? The higher the sales and profits, the higher the value.

Customer Segmentation: Observable Behaviors are the Key

Short of the sales team sharing its internal planning documents, the best the procurement and stakeholder team can do is compare notes on observable behavior. It is vital to include stakeholders in this analysis. They are often treated very differently than Procurement, and the view must reflect the composite of all behaviors.

Attractiveness of the Account		Low	High
	High	**Investment** • Salesperson – often from a technical background or a subject-matter expert in the field; very focused on providing unique, differentiating insights • Typical buying experience – a pleasant experience with additional value-added provided spontaneously. (Beware of the long-term costs associated with managing a more resource-intensive relationship.)	**Key** • Salesperson – a team, headed by an individual with stature in the selling firm (e.g., vice president of key national accounts) • Typical buying experience – very attentive and focused; likely to request regular meetings with some level of transparency
	Low	**Automated** • Salesperson – either no salesperson or a trainee/recent graduate (low value; cannot "hurt" the account) • Typical buying experience – a website or call center with list or list plus pricing and limited availability	**Maintenance** • Salesperson – aggressive, experienced, with a won't-take-no-for-an-answer approach • Typical buying experience – unpleasant; in the realm of regular price increases that are imposed "because they can" versus knowable/acceptable market factors
Customer Segmentation		Low	High
		Value / Profitability of the Account	

Observing behaviors enables the cross-functional team to *develop a hypothesis of how much the supplier values the buying organization.* If there is a disconnect between the seller's behavior and how the buying organization believes it should be ranked, this is a wonderful opportunity for a meeting. Explain the matrix, and ask the salesperson to share how the supplier views the buying organization. (He/she will invariably say as "an Investment" or "Key" because this is the most positive way to portray the relationship.) Explain the inconsistency between the supplier's words and behavior, and ask why this apparent disconnect exists. Sit back and listen to the responses. You are bound to learn something valuable!

After you determine how suppliers are behaving, your next step will depend on the overall layered strategy. Alternatives include either staying in the quadrant or seeking to change the way suppliers perceive the buying organization and moving from one quadrant to another.

Current Quadrant	Observable Supplier Behaviors	*Stay* in this quadrant and do the following...	*Move* to the named quadrant by doing...
Automated	• **Salesperson** – no salesperson or a trainee/recent graduate • **Typical buying experience** – a website or call center with list or list plus pricing and limited availability	• Limit purchases.	**Investment:** • Consider providers who can aggregate products/services (e.g., distributor models). • Consider smaller suppliers for whom the account is more attractive.
Maintenance	• **Salesperson** – aggressive, experienced, with a won't-take-no-for-an-answer approach • **Typical buying experience** – unpleasant; in the realm of imposed price increases	• Extend agreements. • Buy forward. • Manage all forms of risk.	**Investment:** • Pursue specification changes to enable change; open the market to additional competition. *Note: It is possible to transition to Key once the specifications are changed.*
Investment	• **Salesperson** – often from a technical background or a subject-matter expert in the field; very focused on providing differentiating insights • **Typical buying experience** – a pleasant experience with additional value-add provided spontaneously (Beware of the long-term costs associated with managing a more resource-intensive relationship.)	• Extract value from additional services and insights. • Prevent lock-in of supplier-provided specifications through stakeholders (e.g., brands, nonstandard specifications for the category), which lead to maintenance.	**Key:** • If all elements of relationship and the broader requirements of the category strategy align, move to a tighter, more collaborative relationship.
Key	• **Salesperson** – a team headed by an individual with stature in the selling firm (e.g., vice president- key/ national accounts) • **Typical buying experience** – very attentive and focused; likely to request regular meetings with some level of transparency	• Ensure full-value realization consistent with the category and business strategy. • Create and manage joint innovation teams.	**Investment:** • If there is a perceived disconnect between the supplier and access to future value required to deliver on the category strategy, consider moving investment to new suppliers.

Making Your Account More Attractive to Sellers

- Make their jobs easier. Large, global companies can be incredibly bureaucratic and difficult to access, particularly for small, diverse suppliers. Consider steps to reduce this burden.
- Buy from different suppliers. Not all sellers will view your account as key or investment-worthy. What if you purchased from smaller sellers or different points in the supply chain? This approach could easily move your account up in the priority scheme.

Summary

Customer segmentation is a mandatory tool for every category. It requires full participation by the affected stakeholders. Many organizations are focusing on this topic in their sales and business-strategy efforts. As such, customer segmentation is included in most stakeholder-education sessions due to broad applicability to business strategy; stakeholders understand and really appreciate the insights gained from this tool.

Focus on observable behaviors, and don't overthink the results. It is a truism that people do what they are paid to do; this shows up clearly in observable behaviors. We often draw this matrix model on a whiteboard or flip chart in joint buyer/supplier meetings and ask the suppliers to plot where they see the buying organization. They will typically claim "as an Investment" or "Key." The buyers then share the selling behaviors they are seeing—Automated and Maintenance—and the ensuing discussion focuses on the apparent disconnect. This is a very powerful and useful conversation.

CPO Insights from Chris

It is important to watch the way suppliers behave toward you and your organization. Some of these behaviors may result from the way you treat them. As the buyer, if your conduct implies that you are interested in "price only," the customer is going to treat you as "Maintenance" or "Automated." If you truly want to create a partnership relationship and be treated with some respect, you need to invest in the strategic process we have outlined. Determine whether your employees are capable of appropriately managing each supplier and perceiving how the supplier treats you as a customer. There are times, however, when no matter what process you apply, the supplier will treat you as a nuisance. This means you have the wrong supplier.

One question to ask yourself is, "How many suppliers do I have or should I have?" If you find that you are not engaged with key suppliers who are investing in you or see you as key, you have two choices: either change your supply base, or create time to associate with the current supply base.

TEMPLATE: Customer Segmentation

Your Name:	Sub-category:

Attractiveness of the Account			
	High	**Investment**	**Key**
	Low	**Automated**	**Maintenance**
Customer Segmentation		Low	High
		Value / Profitability of the Account	

Y-Axis – Attractiveness of the Account
- Growth potential
- Difficulty to work with
- Payment predictability
- Cache / Reference Value
- Innovation
- Strategic Fit

X-Axis – Value/Profitability of the Account

Current company behavior description and corresponding quadrant (as in C-above, the user will plot the C)	
Objective market view of the sub-category (as in O-above, the user will plot the O)	
Strategic Insights	
Who needs to know these insights?	
• Inside Procurement	
• Outside Procurement	
How will you share the insights?	
Names	**Methods & Core Messages**

13 Strategic Insight Development

Topic Area Assessment Statements

Review these statements from your perspective as a procurement leader. If you "strongly agree" with all of the statements, you may wish to skip to the next topic. But, if you have some doubts about any of them, we recommend that you read this chapter and engage in some self-reflection.

- My team and I use world-class tools to conduct strategic analysis.
- My team and I derive actionable valuable insights from the strategic analysis.
- My team and I communicate strategic insights to stakeholders as we learn them.
- My team and I understand how the various strategic-analysis tools interact.
- My team's and my change-management efforts capitalize on what we have learned across the strategic-analysis tools.

Topic Introduction: Strategic Insight Development

The cornerstones of all strategy development, regardless of the business unit or function, are a compelling vision of the desired end state and an in-depth understanding of the current situation, the competitive landscape, and the capability of the supply base.

1. Strategic analysis of the respective categories is a regular and expected aspect of procurement management.
2. The analysis yields actionable insights. This is not analysis for the sake of analysis. Too many times strategic analysis becomes a "tick-in-the-box" exercise.

It is often said that category management/strategic sourcing is more a change-management process than a procurement process. The reasoning behind this statement is directly related to the change efforts required to implement a layered strategy with stakeholders.

There are numerous strategic-analysis tools in the procurement toolkit. Each is a lens through which to view the supply market, category, and supplier. It is vital, however, to look across the insights gained from using the tools in addition to looking deeply within each tool. The following discussion is focused on the interplay of the trilogy tools that must be used: Category Segmentation, Lean Portfolio, and Customer Segmentation.

Topic-Specific Nomenclature

As in most industries, procurement professionals use a range of terminology with specific definitions. The following terms and definitions are used in this section:

- ***Strategic insight*** – A disconnect between the "as is" practices/behaviors and the "should be" future state that will create value if achieved.

The Tool: Strategic Insight Development

It is an exaggeration to call strategic-insight development a tool; it is more an approach to using the suite of tools. In other words, now that the analysis is performed, we should ask these questions:

- What did we learn?
- What does that mean for our strategy going forward?
- Who must be informed about what we have learned?
- Who must be influenced if our insight is to lead to action?

Answers to these questions form the basis for development of a layered strategy of change, or they presage the resistance that will lead to strategy failure.

This approach to strategic analysis is simple, repeatable, and well proven.

1. Do you understand the current company behavior?

Answer this question logically and dispassionately. If the company is focused on assurance of supply or preventing supply interruptions, both of which result in longer-than-needed contracts, make a note of this. The goal is to accurately reflect the current behavior in a representation on the respective tool.

Example Scenario:

The corrugated-box category with $53M in spend; relatively easy specifications; and a firm, fixed five-year supply contract with a supplier who, although local, does not provide any value-added services or support to you, while this supplier is providing both to other buyers who are demanding more value.

Strategic Insight Development Interpretation – *Buying organization behavior (examples)*

- **Category Segmentation** – Primary concern is securing supply (e.g., a firm, fixed five-year contract); *behavior is consistent with a Proprietary category.*

Number of Sellers with Access to the Intellectual Property			
	More than one (>1)	**Tailored**	**Generic**
	One	**Custom**	**Proprietary** **Corrugate Behavior**
Category Segmentation		One	More than one (>1)
		Number of Customers	

- **Lean Portfolio** – Primary concern is securing supply (e.g., a firm, fixed five-year contract); *behavior consistent with Critical.*

Market Difficulty/ Supply Risk			
	High	**Critical** **Corrugate Behavior**	**Strategic**
	Moderate	**Acquisition**	**Lean**
	Low		**Leverage**
Lean Portfolio		Low	High
		Profit/Spend Impact	

- **Customer Segmentation** – No added value provided for a large customer; *behavior consistent with Maintenance.*

Attractiveness of the Account			
	High	**Investment**	**Key**
	Low	**Automated**	**Maintenance** **Corrugate Behavior**
Customer Segmentation		Low	High
		Value / Profitability of the Account	

2. Do you have an objective view of the market?
Example Scenario:

The corrugated-box category with $53M in spend; relatively easy specifications; and a firm, fixed five-year supply contract with a supplier who, although local, does not provide any value-added services or support to you, while this supplier is providing both to other buyers who are demanding more value.

Strategic Insight Development Interpretation –
An Objective View of the Respective Supply Market (examples)

- **Category Segmentation** – Corrugate, if unimprinted and made to standard sizes, is a generic category.

Number of Sellers with Access to the Intellectual Property			
	More than one (>1)	**Tailored**	**Generic** **Corrugate Market**
	One	**Custom**	**Proprietary**
Category Segmentation		One	More than one (>1)
		Number of Customers	

- **Lean Portfolio** – Corrugate is a classic leverage category unless the supplier and the buyer are engaged in substantial process-improvement activities.

Market Difficulty/ Supply Risk			
	High	**Critical**	**Strategic**
	Moderate	**Acquisition**	**Lean**
	Low		**Leverage** **Corrugate Market**
Lean Portfolio		Low	High
		Profit/Spend Impact	

• **Customer Segmentation** – A corrugate buyer of this scale and predictability

Attractiveness of the Account			
	High	**Investment**	**Key** **Corrugate Market**
	Low	**Automated**	**Maintenance**
Customer Segmentation		Low	High
		Value / Profitability of the Account	

would be a key account, for a rational, local seller.

3. Do you document and act on strategic insights?

Is your current behavior aligned with the market? If so, what will you do to determine that the alignment continues? If not, what will you do to create alignment in the future? Who must be influenced to enable this alignment? What must change internally to allow the alignment?

The answers to these questions inform two processes:

1. **The communication plan** – These insights must be shared with key stakeholders at the same time that they are shared with the team in order to build their strategic understanding of the category. How else can you expect them to approve a strategy that will require change?

2. **The strategic options development process** – Each insight must be reflected/addressed in the strategic options, but it is impossible to remember all of them. Use whatever format works in your situation (from Post-it® notes on a storyboard to cloud-based sourcing systems. The intent is the same: Capture

the insights!).

Strategic Insight Development Interpretation – *Intersection of the Two Views (examples)*

Category Segmentation

- **Behavior** is consistent with a proprietary category.
- **Objective view** – Corrugate, if unimprinted and made to standard sizes, is a generic category.

  Insights – Buyer is behaving in a Proprietary way for a Generic category; substantial value is lost (higher cost/lower value provided). The strategy must address changing stakeholder perceptions of the category.

Number of Sellers with Access to the Intellectual Property	More than one (>1)	**Tailored**	**Generic** **Corrugate Market**
	One	**Custom**	**Proprietary** **Corrugate Behavior**
Category Segmentation		One	More than one (>1)
		Number of Customers	

Lean Portfolio

- **Behavior** is consistent with Critical.
- **Objective view** – Corrugate is a classic Leverage category unless the supplier and the buyer are engaged in substantial process-improvement activities.

  Insights – Buyer's behavior is Critical for a Leverage category; substantial value is lost (higher cost/lower value provided). Are the specifications

Market Difficulty/ Supply Risk	High	**Critical** **Corrugate Behavior**	**Strategic**
	Moderate	**Acquisition**	**Lean**
	Low		**Leverage** **Corrugate Market**
Lean Portfolio		Low	High
		Profit/Spend Impact	

limiting choice? If so, unlocking the specifications is a strategic goal.

Customer Segmentation

- **Behavior (seller)** is consistent with Maintenance.
- **Objective view** – A rational seller would view an account of this size and predictability as Key.

Insights – Seller is treating the account as Maintenance, but the true value is Key. Need to bring in new/potential suppliers to change the dynamic.

<table>
<tr><td rowspan="2">Attractiveness of the Account</td><td>High</td><td>Investment</td><td>Key
Corrugate Market</td></tr>
<tr><td>Low</td><td>Automated</td><td>Maintenance
Corrugate Behavior</td></tr>
<tr><td colspan="2" rowspan="2">Customer Segmentation</td><td>Low</td><td>High</td></tr>
<tr><td colspan="2">Value / Profitability of the Account</td></tr>
</table>

Consider a supplier forum. Make certain that stakeholders understand the insights the implications for change on their part.

The Tool: Strategic Analysis Interplay of the Trilogy Tools

The following is a relatively simple concept. Review what you have learned from each of the three core tools. The process starts with a procurement-centric approach—how the buying organization is behaving in the marketplace versus how the selling organization is behaving toward the buyers—in a comprehensive table/matrix that incorporates all of the elements of each tool.

Trilogy Tool Interaction: Lean Portfolio & Customer Segmentation

- **Lean Portfolio** – How is the buying organization approaching the category?
- **Customer Segmentation** – How is the selling organization behaving toward the buying organization?
- **Strategic Insights/Recommended Intervention(s)**

Lean Portfolio & Customer Segmentation

- **Lean Portfolio** – How is the buying organization approaching the category?
- **Customer Segmentation** – How is the selling organization behaving toward the buying organization?

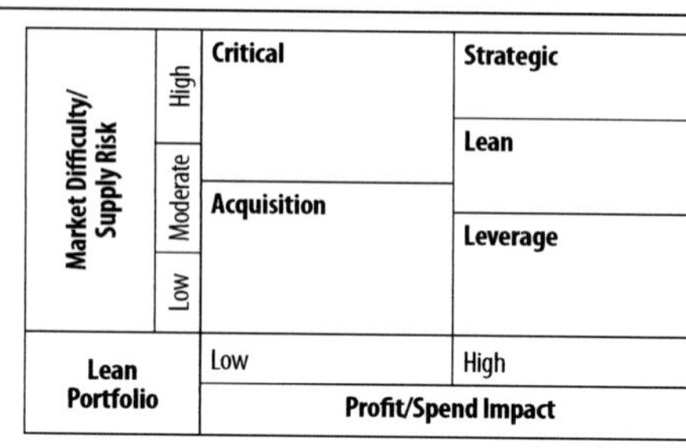

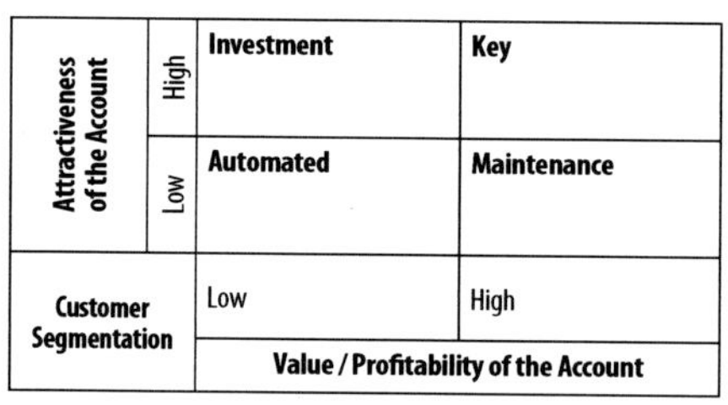

Customer Segmentation	Lean Portfolio: Strategic	Lean	Leverage	Acquisition	Critical
Core					
Investment					
Automated					
Maintenance					

See the following two pages for detailed commentary and recommendations.

Legend	Most favorable to the buyer	Favorable to the buyer	Neutral / Watch out	Unfavorable to the buyer/ Immediate action required	Unlikely

Customer Segmentation	Lean Portfolio: Strategic	Lean	Leverage	Acquisition	Critical
Core	• **Buyer** – driving for sustainable, market-differentiated innovations • **Seller** – aligning for long-term, mutual success • *Establish formal, senior governance to ensure value creation.*	• **Buyer** – driving for process innovation • **Seller** – aligning for long-term, mutual success • *Enable joint continuous improvement; foster additional business opportunities.*	• **Buyer** – establishing market-competitive pricing; moving business periodically • **Seller** – aligning for long-term, mutual success • *Establish clear performance goals and measures based on transparent, realistic business requirements.*	• **Buyer** – simplifying all procurement activities to reduce transaction costs • **Seller** – aligning for long-term, mutual success • *Maintain the relationship at a basic level; offer additional opportunities and references as appropriate.*	• **Buyer** – confirming assurance of supply • **Seller** – aligning for long-term, mutual success • *Initiate efforts to unlock the specifications, and reconnect with the market, while maintaining the relationship.* *Note: This is an exception to our experience and constitutes a breakthrough opportunity.*
Investment	• **Buyer** – pushing for sustainable, market-differentiated Innovations • **Seller** – investing for future opportunities; deploying SMEs to add value • *Enable joint continuous-improvement opportunities.* • *Prevent lock-in of specifications.*	• **Buyer** – driving for process Innovation • **Seller** – investing for future opportunities; deploying System Management Entities (SMEs) to add value • *Ensure value achieved through process Innovations.*	• **Buyer** – establishing market-competitive pricing; moving business periodically • **Seller** –investing for future opportunities; deploying SMEs to add value • *Establish clear performance objectives linked to the business requirements.*	• **Buyer** – simplifying all procurement activities to reduce transaction costs • **Seller** – investing for future opportunities; deploying SMEs to add value • *Maintain the relationship at a basic level; offer additional opportunities and references as appropriate.*	• **Buyer** – ensuring supply • **Seller** – investing for future opportunities; deploying SMEs to add value • *Identify areas of mutual interest; drive continuous improvement / lean initiatives.* *Note: This is an exception to our experience and constitutes a breakthrough opportunity.*

Legend	Most favorable to the buyer	Favorable to the buyer	Neutral / Watch out	Unfavorable to the buyer/ Immediate action required	Unlikely

Customer Segmentation		Lean Portfolio				
		Strategic	**Lean**	**Leverage**	**Acquisition**	**Critical**
Customer Segmentation	**Automated**	• **Buyer** – driving for sustainable, market-differentiated innovations • **Seller** – simplifying selling activities (Web orders/call centers) to reduce selling costs • *Rapidly rethink the relationship; aggressively address internal change barriers.*	• **Buyer** – driving for process Innovation • **Seller** – simplifying selling activities (Web orders/call centers) to reduce selling costs • *Seek supply alternatives; drive competition; change supplier if the relationship does not/cannot improve.*	• **Buyer** – ensuring market-competitive pricing; moving business to another seller periodically • **Seller** – simplifying selling activities (Web orders/call centers) to reduce selling costs • *Seek competition; pursue supplier changes.*	• **Buyer** – simplifying all procurement activities to reduce transaction costs • **Seller** – simplifying selling activities (Web orders/call centers) to reduce selling costs • *Seek supplier alternatives; monitor as needed.*	• **Buyer** – confirming assurance of supply • **Seller** – simplifying selling activities (Web orders/call centers) to reduce selling costs • *Initiate high-priority efforts to change specifications; seek new suppliers.* • *Protect continuity of supply.*
Customer Segmentation	**Maintenance**	• **Buyer** – driving for sustainable, market-differentiated innovations • **Seller** – maximizing account profit by increasing prices/minimizing service • *Initiate high-priority efforts to develop a forward-looking strategy.* • *Rapidly rethink the relationship; aggressively address internal change barriers.*	• **Buyer** – working toward process Innovation • **Seller** – maximizing account profit by increasing prices/minimizing service • *Seek supply alternatives; drive competition; change supplier if the relationship does not/cannot improve.*	• **Buyer** – ensuring market-competitive pricing; moving business periodically • **Seller** –maximizing account profit by increasing prices/ minimizing service • *Seek competition; pursue supplier changes.*	• **Buyer** – simplifying all procurement activities to reduce transaction costs • **Seller** – maximizing account profit by increasing prices/ minimizing service • *Seek supplier alternatives; monitor as needed.*	• **Buyer** – ensuring supply • **Seller** – maximizing account profit by increasing prices/minimizing service • *Initiate high-priority efforts to change specifications; seek new suppliers.* • *Protect continuity of supply.*

Trilogy Tool Interaction: Customer Segmentation & Category Segmentation

- **Customer Segmentation –** How is the selling organization behaving toward the buying organization?
- **Category Segmentation –** How is the buying organization approaching the category?
- **Strategic Insights/Recommended Intervention(s)**

Customer Segmentation & Category Segmentation

- **Customer Segmentation** – How is the selling organization behaving toward the buying organization?
- **Category Segmentation** – How is the buying organization approaching the category?

Attractiveness of the Account			
	High	**Investment**	**Key**
	Low	**Automated**	**Maintenance**
Customer Segmentation		Low	High
		Value / Profitability of the Account	

Number of Sellers with Access to the Intellectual Property			
	More than one (>1)	**Tailored**	**Generic**
	One	**Custom**	**Proprietary**
Category Segmentation		One	More than one (>1)
		Number of Customers	

Category Segmentation	**Customer Segmentation:** Key	Investment	Maintenance	Automated
Custom				
Tailored				
Generic				
Proprietary				

Legend	Most favorable to the buyer	Favorable to the buyer	Neutral / Watch out	Unfavorable to the buyer/ Immediate action required	Unlikely

Category Segmentation		Customer Segmentation: Key	Customer Segmentation: Investment	Customer Segmentation: Maintenance	Customer Segmentation: Automated
	Custom	• **Buyer** – driving for sustainable, market-differentiated innovations • **Seller** – investing to ensure long-term, mutual success • *Very strong alignment of interests (near perfect); allows full access to ideas* • *Be certain that agreements address intellectual-property ownership.*	• **Buyer** – driving for sustainable, market-differentiated innovations • **Seller** – focused on building a long-term, valued relationship • *Good alignment of interests; ensure focus on relevant innovation* • *Ensure ongoing connection to the market and prevent unnecessary lock-in.*	• **Buyer** – driving for sustainable, market-differentiated innovations • **Seller** – focused on minimizing service and maximizing profit • *Extremely poor alignment of interests; results likely to lead to extended lock-in at very high prices with no ownership of intellectual property*	• **Buyer** – driving for sustainable, market-differentiated innovations • **Seller** – focused on minimizing service • *Worst possible alignment of interests; zero likelihood of success* • *Aggressively seek new sources of supply and revisit the forward-looking strategy.*
	Tailored	• **Buyer** – pursuing outstanding service in production/services to buyer's specifications • **Seller** – investing to ensure long-term, mutual success • *Good alignment of interest* • *Highly appropriate when vital materials/products are outsourced* • *Carefully manage the relationship and maintain market surveillance.*	• **Buyer** – pursuing outstanding service in production/services to buyer's specifications • **Seller** – focused on building a long-term, valued relationship • *Good alignment of interests* • *Secure desired process innovations.* • *Protect ongoing intellectual property (process-focused) ownership.* • *Maintain market surveillance.*	• **Buyer** – pursuing outstanding service in production/services to buyer's specifications • **Seller** – focused on minimizing service and maximizing profit • *Poor alignment of interests; service expectations unlikely to be met and ownership of any/all process improvements may be contentious* • *Maintain control of statement of work.* • *Maintain market surveillance.*	• **Buyer** – pursuing outstanding service in production/services to buyer's specifications • **Seller** – focused on minimizing service • *Extremely poor alignment of interests unless the category is simple, perhaps as in small-run (job shop) digital printing* • *Maintain market surveillance.*

Legend	Most favorable to the buyer	Favorable to the buyer	Neutral / Watch out	Unfavorable to the buyer/ Immediate action required	Unlikely

Category Segmentation	Customer Segmentation: Key	Investment	Maintenance	Automated
Generic	• **Buyer** – driving market pricing of readily interchangeable goods and services • **Seller** – investing to ensure long-term, mutual success • *Poor alignment of interests* • *"Over-service" by the selling organization is likely and acceptable if done at no charge.* • *Beware of overcommitment and maintain market flexibility.*	• **Buyer** – driving market pricing of readily interchangeable goods and services • **Seller** – focused on building a long-term, valued relationship • *Poor alignment of interests* • *Over-service by the selling organization is likely.* • *Beware of overcommitment and maintain market flexibility.*	• **Buyer** – driving market pricing of readily interchangeable goods and services • **Seller** – focused on minimizing service and maximizing profit • *Acceptable alignment of interests if (and only if) aggressive market-making steps are taken (such as e-auction) to ensure value is adequate and consistent with the market*	• **Buyer** – driving market pricing of readily interchangeable goods and services • **Seller** – focused on minimizing service • *Poorly aligned interests unless seller participates in an e-auction (or similar) to ensure market-competitive value*
Proprietary	• **Buyer** – ensuring supply of highly restricted goods/ services • **Seller** – investing to ensure long-term, mutual success • *Fortuitous (unlikely but take it!) alignment of interests* • *Ensure that value is appropriate.* • *Seek to understand why viewed as Proprietary from a strategy perspective (can happen with a small company selling a new technology to a large firm; beware of takeovers).* • *Seek to unlock the specifications and broaden the potential marketplace.*	• **Buyer** – ensuring supply of highly restricted goods/ services • **Seller** – focused on building a long-term, valued relationship • *Acceptable (albeit unlikely) alignment of interests* • *Seek to understand why viewed as Key from business strategy perspective (can happen with a small company selling a new technology to a large firm; beware of takeovers).* • *Seek to unlock specifications and broaden the potential marketplace.*	• **Buyer** – ensuring supply of highly restricted goods/services • **Seller** – focused on minimizing service and maximizing profit • *Extremely poor alignment of interests; the buyer is locked in and the seller knows it!* • *Engage stakeholders in efforts to unlock the specifications and develop/implement a forward-looking strategy.*	• **Buyer** – ensuring supply of highly restricted goods/services • **Seller** – focused on minimizing service • *Ensure demand management and compliance measures are in place to limit consumption.* • *Worst possible alignment!* • *Protect short-term supply, and seek new options by engaging stakeholders in efforts to unlock the specifications and develop/implement a forward-looking strategy.*

Trilogy Tool Interaction: Lean Portfolio & Category Segmentation

- **Lean Portfolio** – How is the buying organization approaching the category?
- **Category Segmentation** – What are the fundamental characteristics of the respective supply market?
- **Strategic Insights/Recommended Intervention(s)**

Lean Portfolio & Category Segmentation

- **Lean Portfolio** – How is the buying organization approaching the category?
- **Category Segmentation** – What are the fundamental characteristics of the respective supply market?

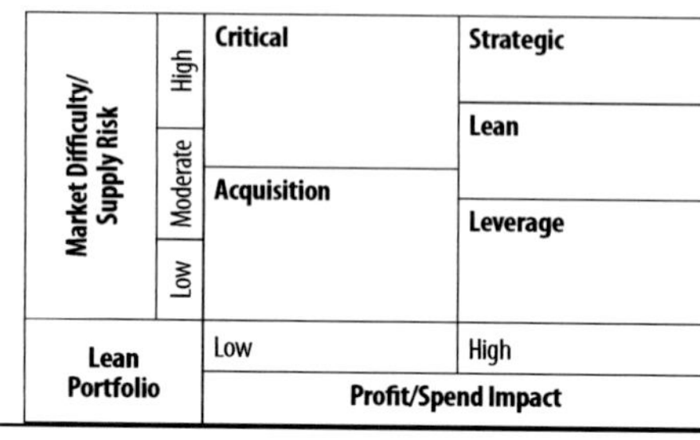

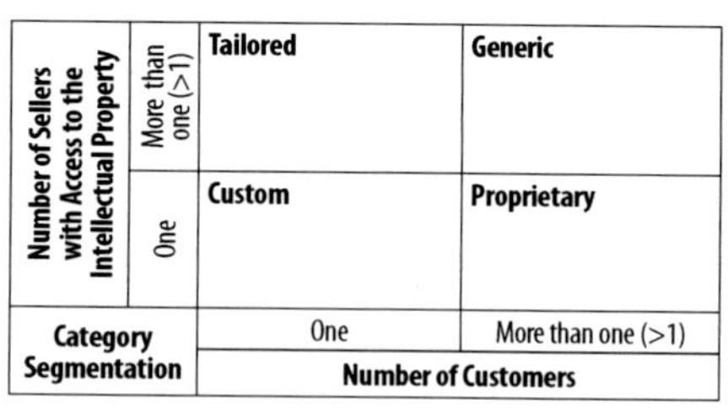

Category Segmentation	Lean Portfolio: Strategic	Lean	Leverage	Acquisition	Critical
Custom					
Tailored					
Generic					
Proprietary					

Legend	Most favorable to the buyer	Favorable to the buyer	Neutral / Watch out	Unfavorable to the buyer – immediate action required	Unlikely

Category Segmentation	Lean Portfolio				
	Strategic	**Lean**	**Leverage**	**Acquisition**	**Critical**
Tailored	• **Buyer** – driving for sustainable, market-differentiated innovations • **Market** – capable suppliers differentiated on service levels (process focused) • *Acceptable alignment of interests* • *Most appropriate when vital materials/ products are outsourced* • *Carefully manage the relationship and maintain market surveillance.*	• **Buyer** – driving for process innovation • **Market** – capable suppliers differentiated on service levels (process focused) • *Good alignment of interests* • *Secure desired process innovations.* • *Protect ongoing intellectual-property (process focused) ownership.* • *Maintain market surveillance.*	• **Buyer** – establishing market-competitive pricing; moving business periodically • **Market** – capable suppliers differentiated on service levels (process focused) • *Good alignment of interests* • *Measure total costs.* • *Maintain ownership of any/all process improvements.* • *Maintain control of statement of work.* • *Maintain market surveillance.*	• **Buyer** – simplifying all procurement activities to reduce transaction costs • **Market** – capable suppliers differentiated on service levels (process focused) • *Acceptable alignment of interests if nature of the relationship is transparent and agreed at arm's length* • *Maintain market surveillance.*	• **Buyer** – ensuring supply • **Market** – capable suppliers differentiated on service levels (process focused) • *Potential for very poor alignment of interests* • *Reestablish ownership of the intellectual property and process improvements (and any transferred assets if applicable).* • *Reestablish control of the statement of work as applicable.* • *Build internal readiness to change suppliers.* • *Develop a forward-looking strategy.*
Generic	• **Buyer** – driving for sustainable, market-differentiated innovations • **Market** – open competition on market-standard goods and services • *Exceptionally poor alignment of interests* • *Revisit buying company strategy.* • *Develop a new, forward-looking business and supply strategy.*	• **Buyer** – driving for process innovation • **Market** – open competition on market-standard goods and services • *Poor alignment of interests* • *Subdivide the category, and review the resulting supply market for potential solutions.* • *Develop a new, forward-looking strategy.*	• **Buyer** – ensuring market-competitive pricing; moving business periodically • **Market** – open competition on market-standard goods and services • *Very strong alignment of interests (near perfect)* • *Ensure market surveillance.* • *Manage shorter-term supply horizons.* • *Move suppliers regularly.*	• **Buyer** – simplifying all procurement activities to reduce transaction costs • **Market** – open competition on market-standard goods and services • *Strong alignment of interests* • *Simplify the entire supply chain to reduce associated costs.* • *Manage shorter-term supply horizons.* • *Move suppliers regularly.*	• **Buyer** – ensuring supply • **Market** – open competition on market-standard goods and services • *Poor alignment of interests with the potential for rapid realignment* • *Aggressively manage stakeholder readiness for change.* • *Pursue unlocking of specifications.* • *Develop and quickly implement a forward-looking strategy.*

Continued on next page

Legend	Most favorable to the buyer	Favorable to the buyer	Neutral / Watch out	Unfavorable to the buyer – immediate action required	Unlikely

		Lean Portfolio				
		Strategic	**Lean**	**Leverage**	**Acquisition**	**Critical**
Category Segmentation	**Proprietary**	• **Buyer** – driving for sustainable, market differentiated innovations • **Market** – monopolized supply based on intellectual property; price and value maximized for seller • *Exceptionally poor alignment of interests* • *Consider purchasing supplier if consistent with broader strategy.* • *Consider make-versus-buy options.* • *Collaborate with stakeholders to develop and implement a forward-looking strategy.*	• **Buyer** – driving for process innovation • **Seller** – maximizing account profit by increasing prices/ minimizing service • *Very poor alignment of interests* • *Protect ownership of all process innovations.* • *Seek to unlock specifications and broaden the potential marketplace.*	• **Buyer** – ensuring market-competitive pricing; moving business periodically • **Seller** – maximizing account profit by increasing prices/ minimizing service • *Very unlikely outcome—limited in practicality to organizations of vastly different scales (i.e. a monopsonistic buyer and a niche seller)*	• **Buyer** – simplifying all procurement activities to reduce transaction costs • **Seller** – maximizing account profit by increasing prices/ minimizing service • *Ensure demand management and compliance measures are in place to limit consumption.* • *Seek supplier alternatives; monitor as needed.*	• **Buyer** – verifying assurance of supply • **Seller** – maximizing account profit by increasing prices/ minimizing service • *The worst possible alignment of interests for the Buyer unless the Seller is particularly altruistic or the balance of the Buyer organization is attractive to the Selling organization* • *Rapidly organize the stakeholders to embrace change and unlock the specifications.* • *Develop and implement a forward-looking strategy.*

Legend	Most favorable to the buyer	Favorable to the buyer	Neutral / Watch out	Unfavorable to the buyer – immediate action required	Unlikely

Category Segmentation		Lean Portfolio				
		Strategic	Lean	Leverage	Acquisition	Critical
	Custom	• **Buyer** – driving for sustainable, market-differentiated innovations • **Market** – creating new and innovative ideas and concepts • *Very strong alignment of interests (near perfect) – ensure full access to ideas* • *Ensure agreements address intellectual property ownership.*	• **Buyer** – driving for process innovation • Market – creating new and innovative ideas and concepts • *Good alignment of interests – ensure focus on relevant innovation* • *Protect ownership of all process innovations.* • *Ensure ongoing connection to the market and prevent unnecessary "lock-in."*	• **Buyer** – ensuring market-competitive pricing; moving business periodically • **Market** – creating new and innovative ideas and concepts • *Marginal alignment of interests – likely to lead to unneeded complexity* • *Seek new sources to prevent "lock-in."*	• **Buyer** – simplifying all procurement activities to reduce transaction costs • **Market**– creating new and innovative ideas and concepts • *Poor alignment of interests* • *Aggressively seek new sources of supply, and revisit the forward-looking strategy.*	• **Buyer** – verifying assurance of supply • **Market** – creating new and innovative ideas and concepts • *Very poor alignment of interests* • *Supplier positioned for extensive (expensive) "lock-in"* • *Aggressively revisit the forward-looking strategy.*

Summary

Strategy development and implementation are the cornerstones of strategic sourcing; every procurement organization with aspirations to world-class performance must have them as core competencies. Strategic-analysis tools are widespread, with each providing a useful view, or lens, for developing new insights. Looking across tools, however, enables profound insight development through the use of additional strategic lenses. These insights provide the motivation to change, both inside and outside of the procurement function. *Never lose sight of inertia; the de facto future strategy is the current strategy until or unless the weight of strategic insights creates the impetus to implement a new strategy.* Insights are valuable when they help stakeholders see the need for change and encourage them to become part of changing current practices to match the desired future state.

Be certain that all stakeholders understand and appreciate the strategic insights as they are developed in the strategic-analysis process. Do not wait until the end of strategy development to share the insights. Be aware that some of the insights will be revealed to the supply base. All organizations "leak" to some extent. This is fine if the suppliers believe you will act on these insights. If you do not act on them, suppliers will see your organization as weak and complacent and will exploit these perceived weaknesses.

CPO Insights from Chris

Insight development is an important aspect of any strategic-analysis tools. It enables the organization to assess its current behavior with an objective market view—in short, to determine if the organization is behaving rationally and competitively in the marketplace.

As you start looking at these tools and how they apply to your situation, you will find a mix of outcomes. In my experience, however, you will always gain new insights when you apply the tools. Business needs change, and supply markets evolve, allowing you to create new opportunities for the company. Timing is also a factor. As the procurement function matures and the company builds trust in your abilities, company leaders will be willing to take more on and build proactive strategies.

14 Risk Analysis

Topic Area Assessment Statements

Review these statements from your perspective as a procurement leader. If you "strongly agree" with all of the statements, you may wish to skip to the next topic. But, if you have some doubts about any of them, we recommend that you read this chapter and engage in some self-reflection.

- My team and I consistently practice category-based risk assessment.
- Stakeholders are aware of the strategic, supply-market consequences of their business decisions.
- My team and I prioritize strategic-risk issues during governance planning with stakeholders.
- My team and I proactively assess and appropriately manage risk associated with layered strategy implementation.

Topic Introduction: Risk Analysis

Risk analysis is at the top of the current procurement and supply-chain agenda and is likely to stay there for the foreseeable future, due to the increasing dependence on long supply chains and continued economic and political instability.

There are two steps in category risk analysis:

1. The first step is to focus on the *risks associated with the current strategy* (including suppliers, design, and production). These risks are the result of internal decision making and the choices business leaders make (or have made in the past). The goal of this analysis is to highlight risk (or, perhaps, its absence) and provide insights that can be used during:
    a. Collaborative spend-governance prioritization and wave planning
    b. Strategy development
    c. Stakeholder communications, while encouraging stakeholders to understand the need to accept change
2. The second step, once a layered strategy is developed, is to *identify and manage implementation risks.*

Procurement is responsible for identifying risks throughout the supply chain; business leaders are responsible for addressing the risks they deem worthy of attention and supporting them with appropriate resources, such as technical staff to enable specification changes and validations. This is often an unsatisfactory situation for procurement professionals because, even when the risks are identified and shared with key stakeholders, little changes. This tool spotlights the risks of current and previous decisions and stresses the call to action.

Topic-Specific Nomenclature

As in most industries, procurement professionals use a range of terminology with specific definitions. The following terms and definitions are used in this section:

- ***None.***

The Tool: Category Risk Analysis

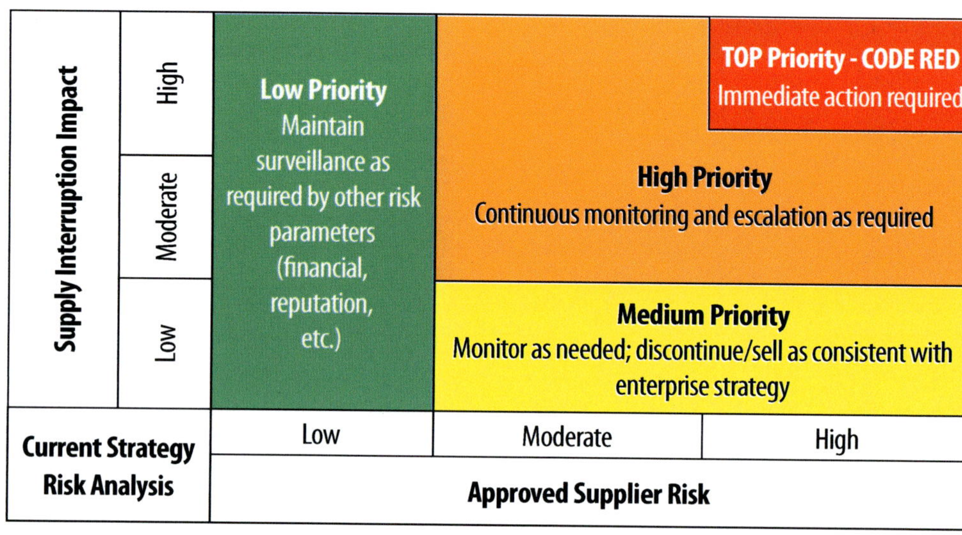

X-Axis – Approved Supplier Risk: The number of currently approved suppliers who are able to produce/supply the current specifications.

- **Low** – Multiple capable suppliers can be approved within a competitive marketplace (generic/leverage).
- **Moderate** – Multiple capable suppliers can be approved without changes to existing designs, processes, licenses, and regulatory approvals and without extensive revalidation.
- **High** – Single source of supply is approved; additional sources cannot be added without substantial product redesign, revalidation, and consultations with end users, who are responsible for any necessary regulatory filings.

Y-Axis – Supply Interruption Impact: The impact on the organization if the approved supply of material fails.

- **Low** – Little to no substantive impact due to amount of material available in the market (substitute products are available).
- **Moderate** – Consumers will notice impact (substitution is possible but will cause some disruptions), and financial markets will increase surveillance of the firm.
- **High** – Extended breach of supply to end customers, which will compromise the reputation of the firm, and/or mandatory regulatory disclosures (e.g., 10K), which may have an adverse effect on the company's financial reputation.

The goal in this analysis is to understand the current situation and highlight the present risks. Too many companies willingly put themselves in situations with highly restricted supply because they view additional sources as unnecessary and a waste of scarce resources.

Current supply risk analysis is a "snapshot" view of the current situation with the current suppliers, specifications, regulatory approvals, and end-customer requirements. To fully understand the risk of the current strategy, it is important to look at the broader supply market. In a crisis, the CEO can muster resources to qualify potential suppliers. If the stability of the company is dependent upon a single supplier, there is a need for an overarching corporate strategy and strategic sourcing to create supply options for the business. Together, these two strategic approaches will create the forward-looking "layered strategy."

The Tool: Strategy Implementation Risk Analysis

The strategic-sourcing process leads to the creation of a layered strategy. Initiation of change leads to a departure from known (or at least knowable) current risks to a host of new implementation risks. The extent of change planned in the layered strategy must reflect both the organization's internal ability to accept and implement the changes and the supply market's capacity to deliver the requisite goods and services. Typically, internal changes are much more difficult and time consuming to implement than external changes. All these changes, however, have attendant risks that vary by strategy element.

Typical layered strategy elements, in order of complexity, include:

- Changing price (from existing suppliers)
- Leveraging existing suppliers
- Reducing the number of approved suppliers (further enhancing leverage)
- Changing the supply base

- Changing internal specifications
- Changing the entire supply chain

Failure (full or partial) at each of these levels results in measurable consequences across:

- The newly created value stream
- The breadth of the business

The Strategy Implementation Risk Analysis matrix addresses these aspects and focuses on proactively dealing with potential issues and the associated risk-management tools required to assure value delivery with minimal risk.

<table>
<tr><td rowspan="3">Relative Value Created / Protected</td><td>High</td><td colspan="2" rowspan="2">Focus – Protect the Value
Be certain that all appropriate plans and tools are used to produce competitive success now and in the future, including protection of process, product intellectual property, and market claims.</td><td rowspan="2">Focus – Prevent Disaster
Assure that prevention and mitigation plans are developed, approved, and ready for proactive deployment.</td></tr>
<tr><td>Moderate</td></tr>
<tr><td>Low</td><td>Rigorous project management</td><td>Tight governance alignment and appropriate project-management tools</td><td>Not appropriate /applicable</td></tr>
<tr><td colspan="2" rowspan="2">Strategy Implementation Risk Analysis</td><td>Low</td><td>Moderate</td><td>High</td></tr>
<tr><td colspan="3">Consequence of Implementation Failure</td></tr>
</table>

X-Axis – Consequence of Implementation Failure: The breadth of impact on the organization when an implementation step fails to proceed as planned.

- **Low** – Focused at the individual level with personal accountability; may lead to reassignment redundancy.
- **Moderate** – Will affect the responsible department or function and cause significant erosion of trust; reorganization is likely to follow.
- **High** – Company-wide impacts on performance and/or perception in the marketplace; change in corporate form (or ownership) may follow.

Y-Axis – Relative Value Created/Protected: The aggregate value being added or protected in the implementation plan.

- **Low** – Minor improvements; typically a "catch-up" to current market parity.
- **Moderate** – Incremental and significant "step changes" in performance that enhance the firm's competitive position and may yield temporary advantages.

- **High** – A breakthrough that unlocks A/RQSCI value and creates a competitive advantage; widespread adoption will permanently transform an industry.

Practical Application – Typical Risk Assessments of Strategy Elements and Recommended Interventions			
Strategy Element and Related Tactics	Value Creation Risks	Failure Risks	Recommendations/Interventions/ Actions
Price changes (from existing suppliers) – (e.g., supplier forum, direct negotiations but *without awarding substantive changes in relative market share)*	• Very Low – Depends on supplier changing invoice pricing and accounts payable changing acceptable pricing	• Very Low – Be sure that promised savings materialize.	• Be certain that new prices and related terms are expressly agreed upon, documented, and implemented fully in both the company and suppliers' systems. • *Note: Successful implementation of this element is likely to lead to complaints to stakeholders from suppliers. Early and effective stakeholder engagement and communication planning is imperative.*
Leveraging existing suppliers – Moving market share within the approved base as a result of negotiations	• Low – Successful changes in this area depend on effective commercial agreements.	• Low – A complete understanding of business requirements is important to ensure that market-share movements (to and from suppliers) do not cause unintended process impacts.	• The more substantive the switch, the more analysis is required. This is balanced, however, by an assessment of the homogeneity of the supply requirement (e.g., US Pharmacopoeia-listed items are interchangeable *per se* if they are listed on the specification, while less-defined products or services warrant more complete analysis to ensure seamless substitution).
Reducing the number of approved suppliers (further enhancing leverage) – Additional movements of market share, including elimination of currently approved suppliers	• Low – Same comments as the previous element but at the next level of rigor required	• May range from low to high. In most cases, it should be low as you are continuing to work with approved suppliers, only fewer of them. Risk of failure could result if there is not a real understanding of the remaining supply base and its capabilities.	• Conduct a complete assessment of the supplier capacity and capability when reducing the number of suppliers. All remaining suppliers must be capable of meeting current and projected requirements.
Changing the supply base – Typically movement to a "low-cost supply base" that leads to "low-cost regional sourcing" (e.g., new geographies)	• Moderate – Securing value in a new environment is more complex than just the price elements; total-cost elements must be considered.	• Moderate – Movement to new sources involves substantive changes to the entire delivery chain and may affect the consumption chain as well.	• From a commercial perspective, negotiations and contracting plans must address the potential cultural nuances reflected in the new sources. Careful and complete understanding of total cost in use, including potential disruptions in the supply chain and consumption chain (regardless of whether product or service), are warranted.

Practical Application – Typical Risk Assessments of Strategy Elements and Recommended Interventions, continued			
Strategy Element and Related Tactics	Value Creation Risks	Failure Risks	Recommendations/Interventions/Actions
Changing the internal specifications – Typically from a company/brand-specific specification to a common industry specification (i.e., functional specification)	• Moderate to High – Changing the specification will raise issues related to change costs (validation, whether a technical function for a product or an in-use function of a service change).	• Moderate to High – While the organization is embracing Lean and Six Sigma, the cross-process impacts of changes in either a service or manufacturing environment are often difficult to predict.	• Piloting the changes is essential! Make proper use of a cross-functional team to develop the changes, assess the potential impacts, and develop mitigation plans. • If the risks are substantial (catastrophic business outcomes are possible), make extensive use of Federal Management Emergency Association (FMEA) and piloting in a controlled environment with appropriate safeguards, as required.
Changing the entire supply chain	• High – As above, with the caveat that absolutely everything is changing.		• As above – Pilot, FMEA, communications plans (including linkages with the corporate disaster plans if appropriate), and complete stakeholder engagement and communications are all necessary.

Summary

Category risk analysis—at the outset of the strategic sourcing on an "as-is" basis and moving forward through layered strategy implementation—is a vital tool to ensure that business leaders understand the attendant risks and value is protected.

Often, the current strategy is deemed to be the low-risk strategy, even if it is based on a sole source of supply. This is false and reflects either complacency or ignorance. Avoid sole sources of supply in all cases where an interruption could have more than a negligible effect on the company. Internal change-implementation resources, such as regulatory, quality, engineering, etc., are not unlimited; but a thoughtful, incremental program to move away from sole-source suppliers can significantly reduce risk to the organization and its bottom line.

Implementation of new strategies should be viewed in the context of what they are replacing. Assess and manage the inherent challenges and risks of the transition to the new strategy. In almost all cases, we recommend doing a pilot implementation. Incorporate the lessons from the pilot into further plans when the implementation progresses.

CPO Insights from Chris

Risk originates in a range of areas within the supply chain. It can be driven by your organization's pursuing a single or sole-sourcing strategy, or it can be driven by the supplier. Risk can arise from emerging and current expectations created by regulations (e.g., conflict minerals, RoHs, REACH). Your company's reputation, however, is linked to your supply base. Ask yourself if you are absolutely sure you would be proud to name your suppliers in public.

The risk of suppliers competing with you in the marketplace is very real. Protect your sales, profit, and intellectual property. Geopolitical risks are pervasive and have the potential to affect supply availability and commodities that, in turn, could have an impact on your bottom line.

As the head of Procurement, you must be certain that the organizational leadership is aware of these risks. It is critical to proactively develop mitigation plans and agreement on future priorities. This is a repetitive, iterative process that will focus on the most critical risk issues at the time. The issues will change over time to reflect the supply market and regulatory/geopolitical environment; the efforts required to address this process should not be underestimated.

TEMPLATE: Risk Assessment, page 1

Your Name:	Sub-category:
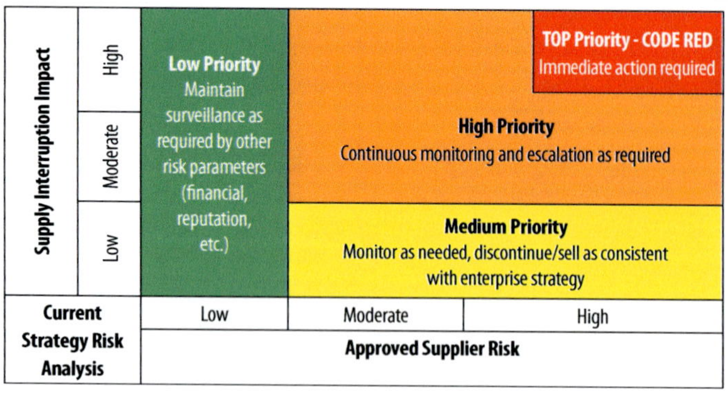	**X-Axis – Approved Supplier Risk:** The number of currently approved suppliers who are able to produce/ supply the current specification. **Y-Axis – Supply Interruption Impact:** The materiality of impact on the organization if the approved supply fails.

Current Strategy Risk Analysis	
Current Strategy Risk Assessment	
Strategic Insights	
Who needs to know these insights?	
• Inside Procurement	
• Outside Procurement	
How will you share the insights?	
Names	**Methods & Core Messages**

TEMPLATE: Risk Assessment, page 2

<table>
<tr><td colspan="6">Your Name:</td><td>Sub-category:</td></tr>
<tr><td rowspan="3">Relative Value Created / Protected</td><td>High</td><td colspan="2" rowspan="2">Focus – Protect the Value
Be certain that all appropriate plans and tools are used to produce competitive success now and in the future, including protection of process, product intellectual property, and market claims.</td><td rowspan="2">Focus – Prevent Disaster
Assure that prevention and mitigation plans are developed, approved, and ready for proactive deployment.</td><td rowspan="5"></td><td rowspan="5">X-Axis – Consequence of Implementation Failure:
The breadth of impact on the organization when an implementation step fails to proceed as planned.

Y-Axis – Relative Value Created/Protected:
The aggregate value being added or protected in the implementation plan.</td></tr>
<tr><td>Moderate</td></tr>
<tr><td>Low</td><td>Rigorous project management</td><td>Tight governance alignment and appropriate project-management tools</td><td>Not appropriate/applicable</td></tr>
<tr><td colspan="2" rowspan="2">Strategy Implementation Risk Analysis</td><td>Low</td><td>Moderate</td><td>High</td></tr>
<tr><td colspan="3">Consequence of Implementation Failure</td></tr>
</table>

Strategy Implementation Risk Analysis	
Future Strategy Risk Assessment	
Strategic Insights	
Who needs to know these insights?	
• Inside Procurement	
• Outside Procurement	
How will you share the insights?	
Names	**Methods & Core Messages**

15 Supplier Negotiations

Topic Area Assessment Statements

Review these statements from your perspective as a procurement leader. If you "strongly agree" with all of the statements, you may wish to skip to the next topic. But, if you have some doubts about any of them, we recommend that you read this chapter and engage in some self-reflection.

- My team and I use an agreed-upon, defined process to plan for and conduct key negotiations.
- My team and I consistently prepare for important supplier negotiations.
- My team and I use the insights from the strategic-analysis tools to prepare for negotiations.
- My team and I view negotiations comprehensively and do not focus solely on "the event."

Topic Introduction: Supplier Negotiations

Conducting supplier negotiations is a core competency in every procurement leader's interactions with suppliers. While procurement leaders may not lead many of the category and sub-category negotiations, they must be ready to help frame and lead strategic supplier deliberations whenever they occur.

Most negotiations, however, are viewed as an event (albeit an important event), and preparations, if any, focus on the tactics and script for the session. Negotiations play a pivotal role in conducting commerce. Certain elements may be addressed in individual sessions, but the broader context of the commercial relationship is established through formal and informal communications between the parties.

The goal of an effective supplier negotiation is to create a sustainable, enforceable relationship that meets the basic needs of both parties. Neither party may be delighted by the outcome, but both must be willing to accept and abide by the resulting agreement.

This section is not intended to supplant formal negotiation training. We believe that all procurement professionals should attend focused negotiation training that includes a robust planning-and-execution framework, practical hands-on application, and video-based feedback.

Topic-Specific Nomenclature

As in most industries, procurement professionals use a range of terminology with specific definitions. The following terms and definitions are used in this section:

- ***MDO – Most Desirable Outcome:*** The best possible outcome of the scenario from the perspective of one of the parties in the negotiation.
- ***LDO – Least Desirable Outcome:*** The minimum that must be achieved by a party to the negotiation in order to conclude a deal.
- ***ZOPA – Zone of Potential Agreement:*** The overlap between the respective parties' MDO and LDO.
- ***BATNA – Best Alternative to a Negotiated Agreement:*** If a ZOPA does not exist, the parties cannot achieve their LDO, and this negotiation will fail to reach an agreement. Then, BATNA becomes their plan to proceed.

The Tool: Supplier Negotiations

The negotiation process is constant. It is punctuated by discrete "events" that receive much of the attention, but it is always occurring. Negotiations are the opportunity to use your insights and demonstrate the internal alignment and clarity (or lack thereof) of the business requirements. Negotiations integrate all of the elements of the sourcing process. Successful negotiations reflect thorough preparation by all parties involved.

Negotiations: The Pre-Game Preparations

Business requirements are fundamental to the negotiation process and must be known before the negotiation commences. The A/RQSCI requirements will be applied directly to the negotiation process. Likewise, sellers are likely to apply a similar, sales-focused construct from their perspective.

Every aspect of the negotiation process must guarantee that the key business needs and the Go/No Go requirements are met. A minimally successful negotiation addresses only these fundamental needs. The fully successful negotiation addresses all of the basic needs and delivers a number of the business wants—the scalable business requirements. The negotiation process may involve trade-offs between the business requirements, but *Procurement's role is to assure that basic needs are never compromised.*

The terminology commonly used to express this is Most Desirable Outcome (MDO) and Least Desirable Outcome (LDO).

A typical approach might look like this.

Business Requirement Parameter	Mandatory Need – The Go/No Go Requirements *(Core to the buyer's LDO)*	The Scalable "Wants" *(Potentially included in buyer's MDO)*
• Assurance of Supply	Required for applicable products/services/ geographies	Optional for expanded range of products/ services/geographies
• Regulatory/Ethical Right to Use	Required for applicable products/services/ geographies	Optional for expanded range of products/ services/geographies
• Quality	Baseline quality measures	Smaller deviation/increased conformance to the specifications
• Service	Minimum acceptable levels	Increased service levels
• Cost	Within acceptable limit; typically based on cost of goods sold (COGS) or budget expectations	Lower costs
• Innovation	Minimum acceptable levels	Preferential access to supplier-created innovation/joint innovation activities

If the selling and buying organizations have an overlap between their respective MDOs and LDOs, this is referred to as a zone of potential agreement (ZOPA). The negotiation process is intended to determine:

1. Whether a ZOPA exists, and if so,
2. Where within the ZOPA the parties will agree to terms.

One last acronym—the Best Alternative to a Negotiated Agreement (BATNA)—is required. Each party must have a valid BATNA upon entering into the negotiation.

The metaphor of a playing field (football/soccer/rugby/hockey) illustrates the competing goals:

<table>
<tr><th>Buyer Goals</th><th>Buyer End Zone</th><th></th><th>Field Position</th></tr>
<tr><td>Buyer BATNA</td><td>Out of bounds for this negotiation</td><td>Seller believes not possible</td><td>0 -10</td></tr>
<tr><td rowspan="8">Buyer's LDO
Acceptable service, quality, innovation, and cost

The Buyer's ZOPA
Highest service, quality, innovation, AND lowest cost

Buyer's MDO</td><td rowspan="8">Mutual ZOPA – the range of potential agreement</td><td rowspan="8">Seller's MDO
Highest possible cost with acceptable service, quality, and innovation

The Seller's ZOPA
Acceptable service, quality, innovation, AND cost

Seller's LDO</td><td>11 - 20</td></tr>
<tr><td>21 - 30</td></tr>
<tr><td>31 - 40</td></tr>
<tr><td>41 - Midfield</td></tr>
<tr><td>Midfield – 41</td></tr>
<tr><td>40 - 31</td></tr>
<tr><td>30 - 21</td></tr>
<tr><td>20 - 11</td></tr>
<tr><td>Buyer believes it is not possible/achievable.</td><td>Out of bounds for this negotiation</td><td>Seller BATNA</td><td>10 - 0</td></tr>
<tr><td></td><td>Seller End Zone</td><td>Seller Goals</td><td></td></tr>
</table>

Each strategic-analysis tool provides insights during the strategy-development-and-implementation process; those same insights should be applied throughout the negotiation process.

- Category Segmentation
  - Where is the category, as viewed from a neutral, objective perspective?
  - How have Procurement and stakeholders in the buying company behaved vis-à-vis this supplier? Are they exercising appropriate leverage?
  - Are stakeholders acting on the strategic insights and enabling change?

- Lean Portfolio
  - Where is the category, as viewed from a neutral, objective perspective?
  - How has the company been behaving?
  - Are stakeholders acting on the strategic insights and enabling change?

- Customer Segmentation
  - How is the supplier behaving now?
  - What messages is the supplier sending?
  - What messages is the buying company sending?

The entire process of developing insights, projecting market-place power and competence, and managing negotiation meetings determines which party achieves more of its most desired outcomes. The above graphic depicts very large ranges for the buyer's and seller's ZOPAs and, therefore, the mutual ZOPA, which is achieved through negotiation. Each party then holds firm or modifies its position. In some instances, the mutual ZOPA is tiny; in others, it is nonexistent. It is important to establish that a mutual ZOPA exists before committing too much time and attention to a particular supplier. The insights to support the existence of a mutual ZOPA are derived through the strategic-sourcing process.

Summary

Negotiations typically start long before most of the participants are aware of what is happening. This is an opportunity for you to remind your team of that fact and to build alignment among stakeholders so that they speak with one voice. Use all strategy-development and stakeholder-engagement activities to reinforce the company's market leverage.

We advocate that you and your team attend formal negotiation training programs that make use of video feedback. There is no substitute for practice and experience, and what the video reveals is irrefutable.

Finally, there are a number of negotiation tactics you can employ, but never use one that could reflect poorly on your organization; your opponents will never forget how you handled the negotiation process.

CPO Insights from Chris

Stakeholders often underestimate the value Procurement brings to negotiations. As a function, we are often seen through the lens of the contract. Buyers become involved for the first time after the negotiations are nearly complete, and it is impossible for them to achieve an optimum outcome.

Most companies provide extensive training for their sales teams on professional selling and negotiation. It is critical for Procurement to provide a similar level of focus and capability on professional buying. Employees must understand the company's needs and convert them into business requirements that lead to a strategy and, ultimately, a negotiation plan. The ability to clearly identify "needs" versus "wants" as part of the planning process is critical.

Procurement leaders recognize the importance of professional training in negotiation. This training can (and, for team-based negotiations, should) include internal stakeholders, as well as procurement professionals. In addition to preparing the procurement team to negotiate with suppliers, the training must also enable appropriate negotiations with the internal stakeholders. Do not underestimate the importance of strengthening these skills and educating business leaders on their roles in the negotiation process. The suppliers will continuously try to bypass procurement professionals and negotiate directly with stakeholders. (Procurement is the professional conduit between suppliers and stakeholders; we are not the police.) Procurement should always be seen as the company's business partner with its best interests at heart.

TEMPLATE: Supplier Negotiations

Your Name:	Sub-category:

Buyer Goals	Buyer End Zone		Field Position
Buyer BATNA	*Out of bounds for this negotiation*	*Seller believes not possible*	0-10
Buyer's LDO Acceptable service, quality, innovation, and cost **The Buyer's ZOPA** Highest service, quality, innovation, AND lowest cost **Buyer's MDO**	***Mutual ZOPA – the range of potential agreement***	**Seller's MDO** Highest possible cost with acceptable service, quality, and innovation **The Seller's ZOPA** Acceptable service, quality, innovation, AND cost **Seller's LDO**	11 - 20 21 - 30 31 - 40 41 - Midfield Midfield – 41 40 - 31 30 - 21 20 - 11
Buyer believes it is not possible/achievable	Out of bounds for this negotiation	**Seller BATNA**	10 - 0
	Seller End Zone	**Seller Goals**	

Negotiation Preparation & Planning

Specific Supplier ______________________

Least Desired Outcomes: A/RQSCI – Needs	
Most Desired Outcomes: A/RQSCI – Wants Prioritize for the concession strategy	
What do we know?	
Prework insights: • Market analysis • Category segmentation • Lean portfolio • Customer segmentation	
Our negotiating team (list the team members)	
The supplier's negotiating team (list who you know/believe is on their team)	
How will you align stakeholders?	
Names	**Methods & Core Messages**
How will you prepare for the negotiation(s)?	
Detailed planning	
Assignment of team roles & responsibilities	
Practice/mock negotiations	

16 Procurement Value Proposition

Topic Area Assessment Statements

Review these statements from your perspective as a procurement leader. If you "strongly agree" with all of the statements, you may wish to skip to the next topic. But, if you have some doubts about any of them, we recommend that you read this chapter and engage in some self-reflection.

- The procurement value proposition reflects the needs of the key stakeholder groups.
- The procurement team consistently and effectively articulates the value proposition of the procurement function.
- Procurement team members can articulate their personal value propositions in a manner that individual stakeholders find engaging and valuable.

Topic Introduction: Value Proposition

> A value proposition is the point at which your company's product/service offer intersects with your customer's desires. It's the magic fit between what you make or do and why people buy it. Your value proposition is the crunch point between business strategy and brand strategy.[1]

The value proposition for Procurement—why it exists (its mission)—is of vital importance. In too many organizations, the mission is simplistic and limited to the basics of tactical supply and cost savings. In progressive organizations, the value proposition includes the entire gamut of value—from assurance of supply through cost, service, quality, risk management, and the exciting area where you start to be seen as a true business partner. Every member of Procurement who interfaces with stakeholders must be able to consistently articulate Procurement's value proposition. This is typically based on a common, generic presentation, but consistency in describing the role of Procurement has value for all concerned.

1. Source: Adapted from Peter J. Thomson's Value Proposition Canvas Template, http://www.peterjthomson.com/2013/11/value-proposition-canvas

The next level of the value-proposition discussion—the individual value proposition—is more nuanced; it asks what is your personal value? This question seems simple, yet the answer must be tailored for each audience.

- Cost-sensitive stakeholders are keen to keep cost at the forefront.
- Research/new-product-development groups are typically focused on access to supply-base innovation.
- Subordinates concentrate on how they will relate to managers over time.
- Peers from other functions are interested in how the "procurement partnership" will take shape.

Every individual's personal value proposition must be consistent with Procurement's value proposition and also include information that applies to that particular person.

Topic-Specific Nomenclature

As in most industries, procurement professionals use a range of terminology with specific definitions. The following terms and definitions are used in this section:

- ***None.***

The Tool: Value Proposition

We highly recommend the value-proposition-development model created by Peter J. Thomson. His model involves building a complete view based on:

- Ideal/target customers
- Discrete service/product offerings

In the case of Procurement, this process occurs at the overall functional level, at discrete subgroup levels (e.g., direct materials, indirect goods and services, R & D, etc.), and at the individual category level. Every member of the procurement team develops a personal value proposition that reflects his/her role in the organization. Everyone must be able to share his/her personal and functional value propositions in a compelling manner. This is a fun and engaging team activity that pays huge dividends with stakeholders!

The Value Proposition Canvas model elegantly juxtaposes your offering and customer expectations to ensure clarity and transparency.

Customer experiences reflect:

- Wants
- Needs
- Fears
- Substitutes

Procurement offerings include:

- Features
- Benefits
- Experiences

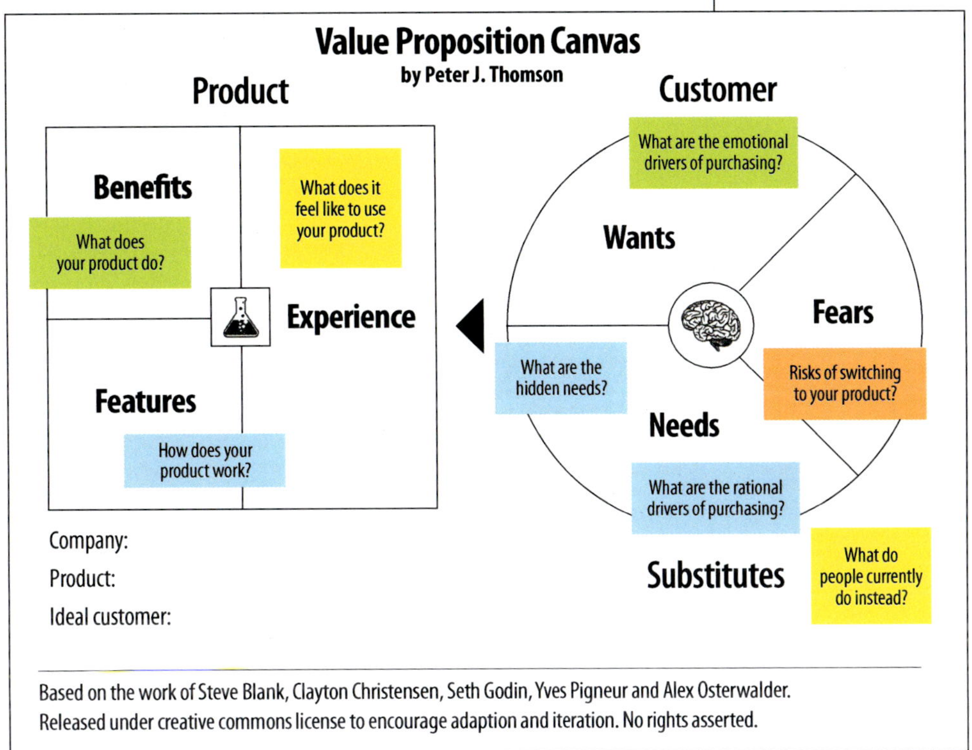

Wants

The emotional drivers of decision making are things that the customer wants to **be, do,** or **have.**

Needs

The customer's needs are the *rational* things that the customer must **be, do,** or **have.**

Fears

The dark side of making a decision is that it carries fear. Customer fears are often the secret reason that no one is buying your service. For any service, there is a subconscious *"pain of switching."* Even if your service/product is better than the competition's, it might not offer sufficient benefits to overcome the inertia of staying with the status quo.

Substitutes

These aren't the obvious competitors; instead, look for the existing *coping behaviors* (e.g., doing the work themselves).

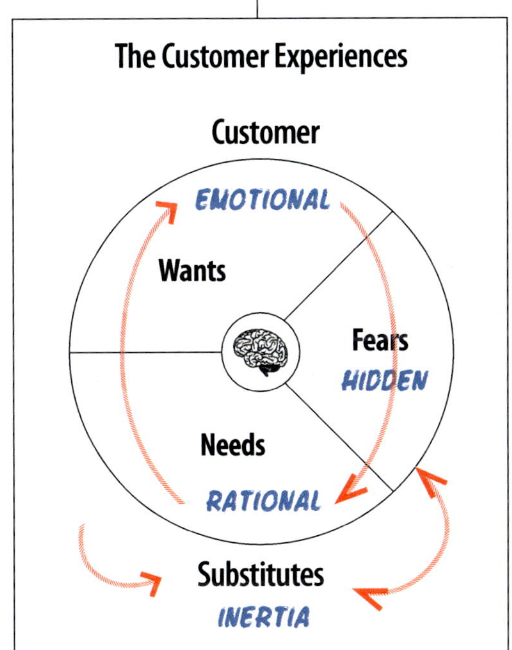

Typical responses by customers will reflect the maturity and capability of the procurement organization and the readiness of the stakeholder community to embrace Procurement.

- **Needs** – The most basic procurement concept—business requirements—is at the core here. It is incumbent upon the sourcing professional to draft the business requirements and ensure that the procurement value proposition will fully meet the underlying business requirements.
- **Wants** – More than the frequent "gold-plating" of specifications, this is most often the supply base they know, the products and services they currently use, the people with whom they are acquainted.
- **Fears** – Change and disruption are the top fears for most customers. It is only *after* the change is successful that we know the typical amount saved through change or the innovation/service/quality benefits that were accessed through change. The long litany of stories about past failed changes will emerge as a potential roadblock. Never forget that stakeholders are, in essence, betting their careers on your supply-chain choices!
- **Substitutes** – The most serious competitors for Procurement are "do-it-yourself" stakeholders who establish shadow-buying and supplier-management organizations. Everybody in an organization views himself as competent to buy the requisite goods or services. Most of us shop online at home; in fact, the new world of electronic, online buying is at least as pervasive in the form of Amazon and other online merchants as it is in the workplace. However, though we may do a good job buying a few items, this hardly prepares us to buy myriad things for a business. There is a big difference between shopping and procurement.

The ultimate test of understanding is to be able to paraphrase what customers are saying to see if you are accurately capturing their intent and needs; in other words, test your value proposition with them and listen. Be sure to adequately address the emotions around fears, as the sharing of fears (typically expressed as concerns) is one of the most honest and transparent moments with stakeholders.

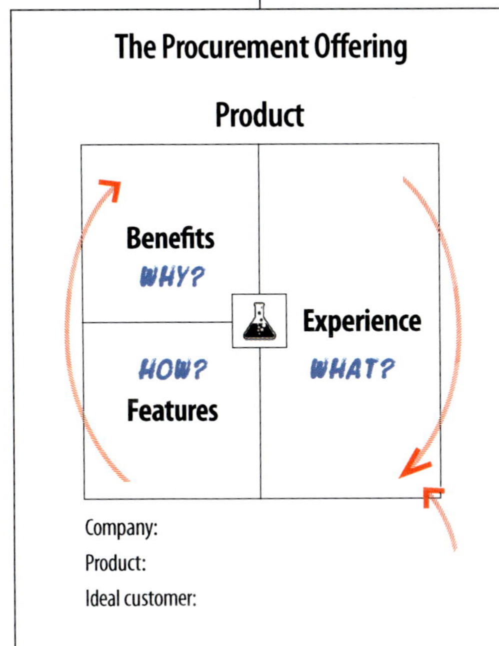

Features

A feature is a factual description of how your product or service works. Features also provide "reasons to believe." But for technology products and innovative new services, important features often add valuable capability.

Benefits

A benefit is what your product or service does for the customer. The benefits are the ways that the features make your customer's life easier by increasing pleasure or decreasing pain. The benefits of your product are the core of your value proposition. The best way to list the benefits of your product or service is to imagine all the ways that it makes your customers' life better.

Experience

Service experience is the way the customer feels about using your service. It is a combination of features and benefits. *Product experience* is different from features and benefits because it is more about the emotional reasons people buy from you.

Product and service features must be expressed in terms that are relevant to customers. This is often a challenge and requires translation from internally focused functional goals to externally expressed concepts. It is necessary to market Procurement to customers.

- **Features** – What will your service or product provide to customers, specifically? Basics, such as global-market access, should not be assumed. List all key features of the sourcing, supply, compliance, supplier management, and payment processes. Most customers will not be aware of the comprehensive range of services Procurement provides.

- **Benefits** – Why are the features of value? Compliant sourcing may not be a feature that is high on the list of all customers (most will assume it to be the case), but it is important to them unless they enjoy lengthy sessions with internal audit. Again, the story to be told here must be compelling and is often unknown at the beginning of the dialogue with stakeholders; you will need to draw this out during the discussion.

- **Experience** – How do you want customers to feel about the service or product you offer? Many procurement organizations work hard to make the transactions easy ("Amazon-like") and ignore the profound stakeholder interactions that are necessary to derive the A/RQSCI requirements. This undervalues Procurement and leads to a supplicant/service mentality. Simple things should be simple; complex and meaningful conversations should be well-orchestrated sessions between professionals.

Developing a comprehensive view of the desired outcomes for customers is a beneficial, individual task at the category level and a team task at the group level. The outcomes are not static and must evolve as new customer requirements emerge.

Summary

Creation of the procurement value proposition is an excellent team-based exercise that should take place when the department is established or reorganized. Revisiting the value proposition should be part of the annual planning process. Developing a personal value proposition and being able to articulate it are excellent small-group exercises. Openly communicate the lessons learned from these exercises. The keys to success are appreciation of the needs of the audience and authentic delivery of your message.

CPO Insights from Chris

A challenge we all face is answering the question, "What is the value proposition that will get you a seat at the table?" Every company is different, and there is no one-size-fits-all answer. Experience shows that you must have capable team members to get a discussion started with the stakeholder community. How you position your associates to be successful with key business leaders is a critical part of the management process.

Elements of a functional value proposition include:

- **Value Delivery to the Business/Stakeholder**–This is not just about price. Our reputation suffers when price is the only driver for performance. We must look at all aspects of value, from the process of converting a requisition to a purchase order to maximizing the benefit across the entire source-to-pay process. You will hear this many times: Cost will usually be rated second or third out of five primary factors (i.e., assurance of supply, quality, cost, service, innovation, and risk). The employee's evaluation will drive his behavior. Encouraging strong results and ways of working create this balance across the business-requirement elements.

- **Delivering Supplier Innovation and Business Evolution** – What are the company's core competencies? Be provocative and challenge assumptions. The quality of the supply base and having the right suppliers are important factors in driving innovation. Suppliers usually need help in bringing innovation into the company. Anything you can do to help them succeed will also make you succeed.
- **Risk** –This applies not only to the risk involved in the products we supply but also to the services we engage in as we outsource more and more.

Success in any of these three areas depends on having capable employees to drive the business and functional agenda. Every procurement associate should be able to explain Procurement's value proposition. Associates who subscribe to and exhibit success behaviors will develop strong relationships with stakeholders and suppliers.

TEMPLATE: Procurement Value Proposition, page 1

Your Name:	Functional Area:
Specific Customer:	Specific Offering:
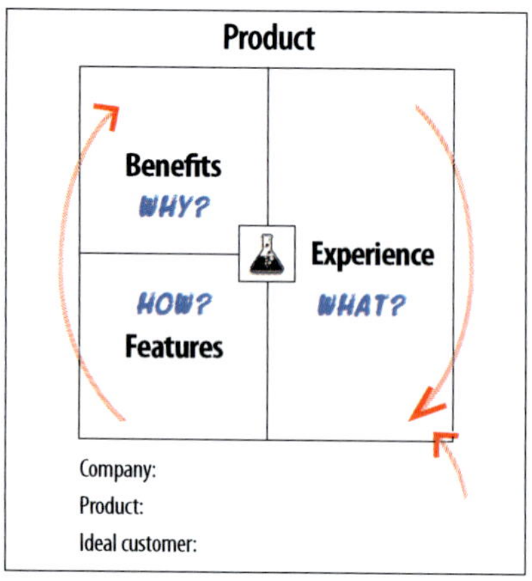	• **Features –** How will your product or service fulfill customers' needs and wants? List all key features of the sourcing, supply, compliance, supplier-management, and payment processes. • **Benefits –** Why are the features of value? How will they make customers' lives better? • **Experience –** What do you want customers to feel about the product or service you offer?

Features	
Benefits	
Experience	

TEMPLATE: Procurement Value Proposition, page 2

Your Name:	Functional Area:
Specific Customer:	Specific Offering:

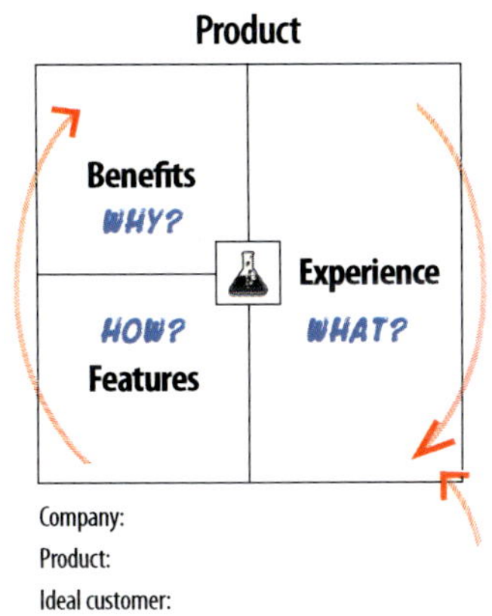

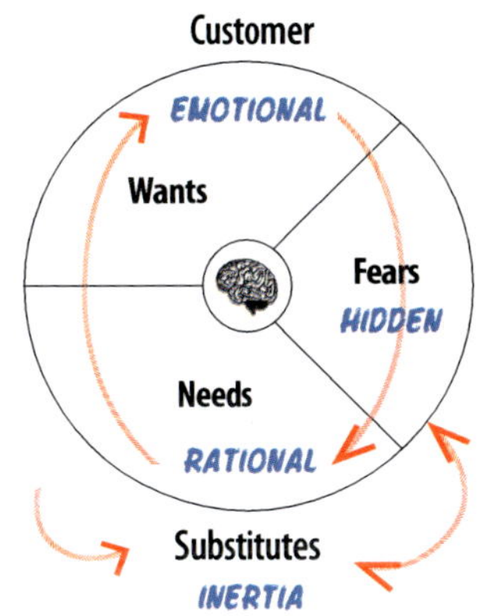

Draft a script that puts the customer situation together with your product or service in a compelling way.	
Proactively address customer concerns; leave no space to resist. (Give customers a reason to say "yes.")	
Be sure that the benefits of your offering are tangible and valuable to your customers; phrase benefits in terms that matter to them.	

Practice the delivery, and simplify to keep to the bare minimum necessary to convey the message.
Build in feedback as you apply the technique value proposition development and refinement approach.

17 Stakeholder Engagement

Topic Area Assessment Statements

Review these statements from your perspective as a procurement leader. If you "strongly agree" with all of the statements, you may wish to skip to the next topic. But, if you have some doubts about any of them, we recommend that you read this chapter and engage in some self-reflection.

- The procurement team actively maps and manages key stakeholders.
- Everyone in Procurement makes stakeholder engagement a high priority.
- Stakeholder engagement activities reflect Procurement's change-management priorities and categories.

Topic Introduction: Stakeholder Engagement

Stakeholder engagement is the cornerstone of effective procurement. In short, the budget holders must positively and effectively participate in the relationship in order to achieve success. The first steps in this process are to identify the key stakeholders and then understand the starting point for the relationship. This process is applicable at all levels of Procurement, beginning with the CPO, his team, and their peers across the executive levels of the organization.

Stakeholder Perceived Value from Procurement		Low	High
	High	***Potential Ally*** *(Pleasant surprise – "I didn't know you could. . .)*	***Real Partner*** *(Openly working together to create mutual value)*
	Low	***Avoid*** *(Avoid them whenever possible)*	***Necessary Evil*** *(The minimum necessary to ensure compliance)*
		Low	**High**
		Stakeholder Perceived Need for/Requirement to Use Procurement	

Procurement leaders strive to create real allies and partners. You *never* want to be avoided or thought of as a "necessary evil."

Some mapping approaches assign negative labels to stakeholders, such as "blockers" or "avoiders." These are not helpful and can backfire if stakeholders learn of their label. We prefer to focus on the stakeholders' behaviors toward the procurement agenda and value proposition. As such, we are not seeking to "read their minds"; we are simply interpreting their actions, which we can use as a basis for further discussion.

The other important element of our approach is to recognize that organizational influence, while often linked with organizational stature, is more often a reflection of individuals within the organization. Some people are respected and listened to because they are senior leaders. Others are respected and trusted because of their knowledge and experience. Every organization has comparatively low-level staff members who are subject-matter experts on particular topics and to whom others defer when they are seeking opinions on those subjects.

The goal is to focus on "key stakeholders"—the critical few internal staff members who can either directly stop an initiative by exercising their formal decision-making rights or indirectly slow an initiative through endless data requests (e.g., filibustering the topic to death). Depending on the size of the organization, this number is not often in the hundreds; it is more likely to be under one hundred. But the number of key stakeholders must reflect the mapping and your analysis of their degree of support (or resistance). Don't let the desire to manage a small group of stakeholders influence your assessment and thereby omit many key people.

Process warning: Stakeholder mapping is inherently personal and must be treated with complete confidentiality. The goal is to build effective relationships by increasing stakeholders' understanding and appreciation of the procurement value proposition and functional strategy.

Topic-Specific Nomenclature

As in most industries, procurement professionals use a range of terminology with specific definitions. The following terms and definitions are used in this section:

- ***Stakeholder mapping*** – The process of reviewing the observable behavior of stakeholders and your perceptions of the degree to which they are supportive of your efforts

The Tool: Stakeholder Mapping

The process starts with the identification of the key stakeholders. First, identify individual stakeholders by name. It is not sufficient to list categories of people, such as plant managers, as each person should be treated as a unique individual.

1	9	17	25
2	10	18	26
3			
4			
5			
6			
7	15	23	31
8	16	24	32

First step – List all affected stakeholders and associate the name with a number.

Associating names with numbers enables number plotting, which further protects the confidentiality of the process.

While the process is to use names first, to prevent an inordinate focus on names, it is typical to convert names to numbers for the plotting process.

Note: Different work groups often repeat this process. Typically, the procurement leadership team will conduct an analysis, but a category team may include some of the same stakeholders. If common stakeholders are identified, then assign a primary procurement contact to such stakeholders.

The initial goal of the mapping process is to understand the "as-is" situation. How are stakeholders behaving at this moment?

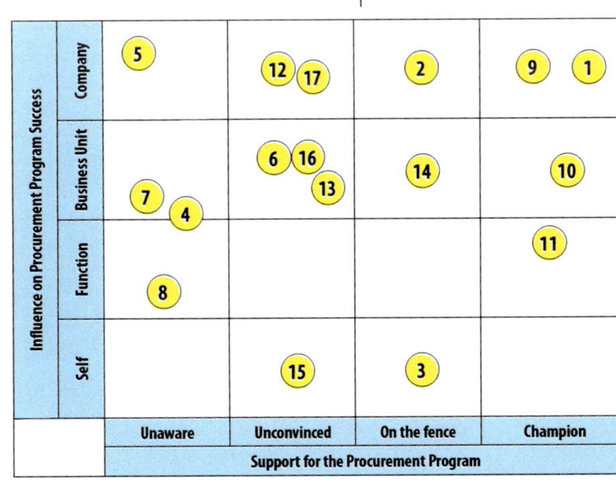

This analysis results in the creation of a picture of support and serves as the basis for planning focused interventions.

Many groups fail to move beyond the "as-is" model. The purpose of the "as-is" model is to understand the current situation and the degree of difficulty required to achieve the "to-be" model.

The "to-be" model results from identifying those who must be supportive of the procurement agenda in order to guarantee success.

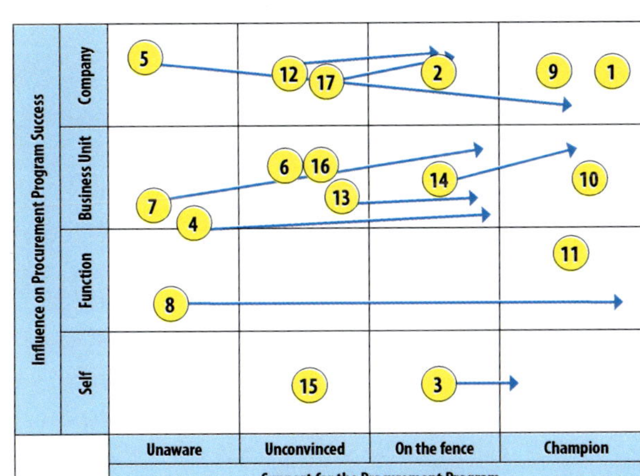

This depiction shows specific individuals moving from left to right in recognition of their increased support.

The main question is *how*? *How* will you encourage them to change their attitudes and beliefs and support your efforts? *Who else* can help with this change process?

The answer has two parts. First, assess each person in terms of motivation, and tailor your individual approach to build his/her understanding and support of the procurement agenda. This may sound overwhelming, but there are always common approaches that will effectively address multiple stakeholders. Second, the procurement person is never alone; the current "champions" can be drafted, if they are effectively scripted or guided, to help move others along the support continuum. These actions are the essence of the stakeholder-engagement plan.

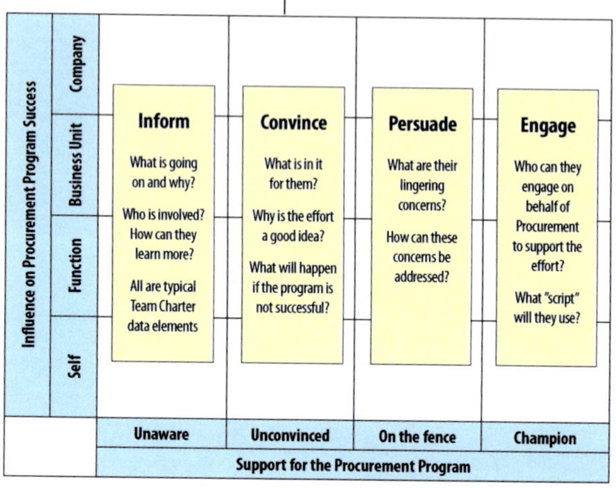

The Tool: Stakeholder Engagement Planning

The plan lists the stakeholders: their "as-is" and "to-be" status; and, specifically, how you propose to increase their level of support. The people responsible for the interventions must be listed, and any preparation plans or scripts must be created in advance.

To Whom	What to Communicate	Method
Sponsor	Project updates, key milestones, resource needs, issues.	Face-to-face, phone, teleconference
Champion Stakeholders	Project updates, key milestones; seek their support.	Face-to-face, phone, teleconference
Unaware Stakeholders	Create awareness; conduct informational sessions.	Face-to-face initially; then, by their preferred method
On-the-fence Stakeholders	Determine and understand significant questions and areas of concern.	Face-to-face until level of buy-in indicates other methods are appropriate
Unconvinced Stakeholders	Seek and understand reasons for resistance; determine what is needed to resolve/mitigate concerns.	Face-to-face, until level of buy-in indicates other methods are appropriate
Team Members	Updates, action items, key milestones, review of data, etc.	Face-to-face; email

Summary

If this process sounds intensive, that's not surprising. It is involved and deeply personal. Stakeholder engagement is the absolute cornerstone of effective procurement (at all levels) and the differentiator between excellent and mediocre procurement efforts. Many procurement organizations that bemoan a lack of top-down direction and support are invariably underplaying Procurement's role and hoping that the CEO/CFO will create a mandate to engage Procurement on procurement-dictated terms (ironically seeking to make Procurement a "necessary evil"). Even in organizations with more of a top-down culture, this is never sufficient. Success emanates from a positive appreciation of the procurement value proposition and a "pull" from stakeholders.

This process is not static. As individuals change roles, their assessments and engagement plans must evolve as well. The great news is that, as this process is practiced, it becomes second nature and can be rapidly updated.

CPO Insights from Chris

Procurement's functional success depends upon the stakeholder community's trust. Trust takes time to build but can be destroyed overnight. It is easy to underestimate the time and effort Procurement must spend in understanding and building the relationship with the stakeholder community. Procurement is not a sales function externally, but internally, an important part of the leadership role is to ensure that the value proposition meets stakeholders' needs.

To be successful, the questions you need to answer are:

- Do you know who the key stakeholders are?
- Do you know which stakeholders can make you successful? Block or hinder your success?
- How will you or your team engage with these stakeholders?
- How do you keep track of the needs of the stakeholders to stay current with and meet their needs?
- How do you gauge your success in developing their engagement?

Stakeholder mapping is a critical component of leadership. Sometimes, the stakeholders are suppliers with strong relationships within the company. These suppliers can be a thorn in your side while you are moving toward internal success and trust. Engagement with stakeholders results in a contract based on understanding their needs and putting in place mechanisms to report how you are meeting those needs. Do not underestimate the importance of stakeholders' style and culture and how you proactively engage with them in a manner that is consistent with their preferences. Success depends upon recognizing that each person is distinctive and incorporating that understanding into your engagement plans.

TEMPLATE: Stakeholder Engagement, page 1

<table>
<tr><td colspan="4">Your Name:</td><td colspan="3">Functional Area:</td></tr>
<tr><td rowspan="2">Step #1 – List stakeholders
(Focus on internal stakeholders)</td><td colspan="3">Name</td><td colspan="3">Role</td></tr>
<tr><td colspan="3"></td><td colspan="3"></td></tr>
<tr><td rowspan="6">Step #2 – Plot the stakeholders based on current behavior/feedback</td><td rowspan="4">Influence on Procurement Program Success</td><td>Company-wide</td><td></td><td></td><td></td><td></td></tr>
<tr><td>Business unit</td><td></td><td></td><td></td><td></td></tr>
<tr><td>Function</td><td></td><td></td><td></td><td></td></tr>
<tr><td>Self</td><td></td><td></td><td></td><td></td></tr>
<tr><td colspan="2" rowspan="2">The "as is" Stakeholder Map</td><td>Unaware</td><td>Unconvinced</td><td>On the Fence</td><td>Champion</td></tr>
<tr><td colspan="4">Support for the Procurement Program</td></tr>
</table>

TEMPLATE: Stakeholder Engagement, page 2

<table>
<tr><td colspan="3">Your Name:</td><td>Functional Area:</td></tr>
<tr><td rowspan="6">Step #3 – Act on the Results</td><td>Assessment (by name)</td><td>Why is this person supportive, unsupportive, or unaware?</td><td>How can he/she help you with others?
How will you address his/her needs,
and who can help you do it (e.g., the champions)?</td></tr>
<tr><td>Champions</td><td></td><td></td></tr>
<tr><td>On the Fence</td><td></td><td></td></tr>
<tr><td>Unconvinced</td><td></td><td></td></tr>
<tr><td>Unaware</td><td></td><td></td></tr>
</table>

18 Stakeholder and Supplier Feedback

Topic Area Assessment Statements

Review these statements from your perspective as a procurement leader. If you "strongly agree" with all of the statements, you may wish to skip to the next topic. But, if you have some doubts about any of them, we recommend that you read this chapter and engage in some self-reflection.

- My team and I know the extent to which current suppliers are satisfied with Procurement.
- My team and I consistently assess stakeholder satisfaction.
- My team and I know the state of supplier satisfaction with the broader commercial relationship—the mix of price, service demands, feedback provided, payment terms, access to stakeholders—with the company.
- Feedback loops are continuous and transparent.

Topic Introduction: Stakeholder and Supplier Feedback

Procurement is a service function; feedback is the most essential element in measuring success. Feedback is described by many as a gift; sometimes, it is a gift you want and, sometimes, not. In either case, it is essential to improvement. Feedback should be a candid reflection of how key constituents perceive and feel about the service they receive. For that reason, it is important to regularly survey the two core constituencies of procurement—internal stakeholders and external suppliers. The techniques are similar, but the approaches are necessarily different.

Your goal with stakeholders is to establish a close, rather than an arm's-length, relationship. Stakeholder relationships are governed by personal contracts and, occasionally, by service-level agreements. Supplier relationships, no matter how strategic in nature, must always be based on explicit commercial terms. The supplier-feedback process seeks to augment this commercial relationship but must not inadvertently displace or redefine the basic commercial terms. The most important parts of receiving feedback, however, are constant acknowledgment and appreciation of the input and then following up in a timely fashion.

Internal stakeholders are addressed through three primary means: personal interviews (internal or through a third party), focus groups, and surveys (electronic or hard copy). External suppliers are typically addressed through direct interviews by internal or external staff (limited to the "top-tier" suppliers) and electronic surveys.

Before collecting any input, the recipients of the input must commit to providing timely feedback. It is worse to collect actionable input and not act on it than to never collect the information in the first place. Collecting input establishes an expectation that you will act. Do not disappoint anyone who takes the time to provide feedback!

Topic-Specific Nomenclature

As in most industries, procurement professionals use a range of terminology with specific definitions. The following terms and definitions are used in this section:

- ***Likert scale*** – A survey evaluation scale where respondents specify their level of agreement or disagreement on a symmetric agree-disagree scale for a series of statements

The Tool: Internal Stakeholder Feedback Collection

The feedback process starts with the stakeholder-mapping exercise presented in Chapter 17 to identify the key stakeholders.

In-person reviews, which are typically conducted at the most senior levels of the organization, are opportunities to collect and understand stakeholder input *and* to clarify the procurement value proposition. If possible, conduct these extremely important two-way conversations in person. If that is not feasible, the next-best option is video conferencing; the third is to have the discussion by phone.

Many procurement leaders prefer to use members of the procurement leadership team to conduct these sessions. If the team is comfortable in this role and able to relate to stakeholders on an "adult-adult" basis, as described by author Virginia Satir in *Peoplemaking*, this is indeed the best arrangement. In-person conversations solidify the relationship and extend the basis of trust. If, however, any members of the procurement leadership team are more likely to conduct the dialogue from the perspective of "parent-child," they should not proceed. The interview will not go well, feedback will be flawed, and the basis of mutual trust and respect will not be established. In such cases, it is best to use a trusted third party who is sufficiently briefed on the procurement function.

Typical Stakeholder Engagement Questions

Agree/Disagree Questions:

Using a Likert Scale, evaluate the extent to which respondents agree or disagree that Procurement is effective at:

1. Achieving important business results
2. Understanding the key business priorities
3. Aligning procurement activities to support the key business priorities
4. Presenting useful supply options/opportunities that will improve business performance
5. Communicating with the company
6. Developing internal (company) relationships
7. Developing external (suppliers, etc.) relationships

Open-Ended Questions:

8. What actions or activities would you like Procurement to increase?
9. What actions or activities would you like Procurement to decrease?
10. What else would you like to share?
11. Is there any one associate, group, or team within Procurement you would like to recognize?
12. How would you like to receive feedback on this survey? Options include group email, personal email, group presentation, one-to-one review, in person, or phone call.

Regardless of whether these discussions are conducted by procurement leaders or a trusted third party, they must be based on listening to and understanding the stakeholder. Whoever conducts these meetings, that person should never be defensive or argumentative.

Focus groups are another way of collecting stakeholder feedback (and sharing the procurement value proposition). The key advantage of focus groups is the inclusion of more participants in the same amount of time. The disadvantages or risks are that they require a highly skilled facilitator to prevent a minority opinion from becoming the de facto group opinion. Either HR staff or a third party typically conducts focus groups.

Internal surveys are widely used since the advent of simple-to-use tools, such as Survey Monkey, SurveyGizmo, Zoomerang, and other similar sites.

The advantages of electronic surveys are very low administrative costs and rapid turnaround. The disadvantages can include poorly constructed questions, inappropriate target audiences, failure to understand and calculate the significance of responses, and over-surveying of the same people. We strongly recommend that you use the standard five-point rating scale known as a Likert scale. Most organizations have internal experts available to assist with survey design. Use them.

The Tool: Supplier Feedback Collection

Supplier feedback is different from stakeholder feedback. The supplier is in a commercial relationship with your company and may or may not be completely fulfilling all requirements or the potential for a relationship. Too many companies accept inadequate supplier relationships that could, with a little open and actionable feedback, be transformed into meaningful relationships. This is vital in relationships that are dependent on the world of ideas—Marketing, Research, and Engineering, to name a few. Suppliers who believe their ideas are valued and are treated as an extension of the company will contribute their best efforts. Those who are ignored (or worse) will fulfill their contractual obligations, but your competition is likely to receive their best efforts.

Most procurement organizations express their vision as the desire to be "the preferred customer for the best suppliers." It is an excellent vision. It is also extraordinarily difficult to achieve. Such a vision statement requires some form of ongoing feedback to gauge progress (in addition to the expected market surveillance and strategic-analysis efforts as part of strategic sourcing).

Personal supplier interviews are appropriate for the very top of the supply base. Identifying these "critical few" suppliers is part of the supplier-segmentation process typically conducted in strategic-sourcing and supplier-value management. In very few cases will there be more than twenty-five suppliers included in this process.

Once you identify the suppliers you wish to include in the survey, you should discuss your intention to do so with the appropriate stakeholders (a great use of the relevant governance body). While Procurement leads and "owns" commercial relationships, the broader relationships at this level are very important and may include your company's executives. It is highly inappropriate to survey suppliers without prior stakeholder involvement and agreement. In selected cases, stakeholders may participate with Procurement in the dialogue. *Note: If this is to occur, the level of planning and preparation expands exponentially, as it will require practice sessions (typically recorded and reviewed by the team that will conduct the supplier interviews).*

Typical Supplier Questions

A selection of typical supplier questions is usually based on one or more of the following conditions:

1. The parameters of customer satisfaction are clearly established and achievable.
2. The customer is pushing your organization to improve the level of quality you provide.
3. The customer is pushing your organization to lower your total costs.
4. The customer is pushing your organization to improve delivery or service.
5. The customer is supportive of your commercial requirements.

These conditions should be structured using both the Likert scale and open-ended response opportunities. *Note: In many cases, suppliers will be tempted to skew their responses to the positive end of the spectrum to avoid perceived (or real) repercussions. To avoid this tendency, particularly in important, trust-based relationships, use an external firm in the beginning to collect data until a track record of trust and collaboration is established.*

Try to prevent or avoid "halo or horn" effects that may result from any recent changes, such as changing payment terms across the supply base. If you recently introduced substantive changes in any of your terms, discontinued products, or moved business to new suppliers, the results are likely to be affected. Beware of overreading the results in these cases.

Electronic surveys are easy to use, and the same guidelines apply to internal and external suppliers. The fundamental goal of the discussions is to understand the relative value delivered to the company by the supplier versus (1) what the company needs and (2) what the supplier is capable of delivering. The question remains: Is the company the best customer of the best suppliers?

Summary

Remember, "feedback is a gift." You are better informed with it than without it. Stakeholder and supplier feedback should always lead to deeper insights and actions and be followed up with thoughtful communications. The process leads to deeper understanding and trust, both of which enable the procurement value proposition.

CPO Insights from Chris

The foundation of success for a procurement function that wants to be seen as a true partner of the company is to actively seek feedback and then act with integrity on what you learn. The maturity of the function—the extent to which the procurement value proposition has evolved from a low-value service provider to a high-value commercial partner—will dictate the type of feedback you are seeking (internal to the function, internal to the company, or external).

Internal to the Procurement Function: Procurement Team Members

There are numerous ways to acquire feedback on how Procurement is perceived. If you have a motivated workforce, you can be successful at engaging with the internal stakeholders and external suppliers. We use small focus groups facilitated by our HR partner (or a neutral third party who has no interest in the information that is shared). The process permits participants to discuss a range of topics, such as:

- Jobs and day-to-day activities
- Communications
- Commitment to your organization and its goals
- Organization leadership
- Satisfaction of your employees

Instruct the facilitator to ask questions that reveal what is working, what needs improvement, what the opportunities are, and what the participants can do differently. The keys to success are confidentiality and trust in the facilitator; employees must feel comfortable in order to be open with their feedback. The facilitator has to be able to consolidate the feedback and identify the trends/themes that procurement leaders must address. Employees will play a role in this process by sharing responsibility for the improvements.

I have had great success with this process. We obtain both positive and negative feedback and act as a leadership team to address concerns. It is part of the toolkit to involve and engage our associates. When I compare this process to Gallup,[1] the focus-group process gets to the root of the issues more quickly and in a more transparent fashion. Of course, Procurement's leader(s) must be willing to take action where the feedback is actionable.

1. Previously BD used the Gallup Q12 process.

External to the Procurement Function: Managing the Organizational Matrix

What is the reality of managing the matrix in global corporations? Lines of authority are rarely clear or simple; modern organizations are highly interdependent. One of the constant challenges most procurement functions face is navigating the stakeholder community—listening to and building trust with your stakeholders. I have used a range of techniques to stay connected with the matrix. Many of them are not new; the key is to be consistent and persistent.

- Survey – Once or twice a year, solicit feedback on how the procurement function is performing. Communicate findings to the participants and your leadership team, and follow up with action.
- Every two years, interview the top twenty to thirty leaders of the company, including the CEO or chairman. This is powerful in terms of gaining insight. Use a third party to get a balanced view. When you communicate the results to the participants, do it face to face. Be sure that they know that you understand the feedback, value their time and insights, and will act on feedback appropriately.
- Be certain that you and your team are talking to the correct stakeholders about topics that interest them. Look at tools to capture this information so that it can be shared within Procurement. Be clear on the value proposition.
- Establish a cross-business team—a steering team or purchasing council—so that you can bring ideas to the table and guarantee that they would work for the company.

The matrix is a challenge. Sustaining engagement and following up are key to building trust.

TEMPLATE: Model Stakeholder Survey

Date	**Stakeholder area** (business/function/ region)
Stakeholder name	**Stakeholder role/title**

Do you agree or disagree that Procurement is effective at:	**Agree**	**Partially Agree**	**Neutral**	**Partially Disagree**	**Disagree**
• Achieving important business results					
• Understanding key business priorities					
• Aligning procurement activities to support the key business priorities					
• Presenting useful supply options/ opportunities that will improve business performance					
• Communicating with the company					
• Developing internal (company) relationships					
• Developing external (suppliers, etc.) relationships					

Open-ended questions	
• What actions or activities would you like Procurement to increase?	
• What actions or activities would you like Procurement to decrease?	
• What else would you like to share?	
• Is there any one employee, group, or team within Procurement you would like to recognize?	
• How would you like to receive feedback on this survey? (give suggestions/options)	

TEMPLATE: Model Supplier Survey

Date	Supplier company name
Supplier respondent name	**Supplier respondent role/title**

Do you agree or disagree that (our company) is effective at:	Agree	Partially Agree	Neutral	Partially Disagree	Disagree
• Pushing your organization to improve the level of quality you provide					
• Pushing your organization to improve your total costs					
• Pushing your organization to improve delivery or service					
• Supporting your commercial requirements					
• Creating a mutually satisfying relationship					

Open-ended questions	
• Is our company your most preferred customer? If yes, why? If not, why not?	
• What are the characteristics of your ideal customer relationship? How does our relationship compare?	
• Within your company's customer-segmentation model, where does (our company) fit?	
• What else do you want to share about our relationship?	
• How would you like to receive feedback on this survey?	

19 Trust

Topic Area Assessment Statements

Review these statements from your perspective as a procurement leader. If you "strongly agree" with all of the statements, you may wish to skip to the next topic. But, if you have some doubts about any of them, we recommend that you read this chapter and engage in some self-reflection.

- Stakeholders trust Procurement to understand and represent their business interests.
- Procurement team members trust the functional leaders to accurately represent their business requirements.
- Procurement team members proactively build trust-based relationships with priority stakeholders.

Topic Introduction: Trust

Trust? Why is the topic of trust in *The Global Procurement Leader's Handbook*? Trust matters in all aspects of human endeavor; yet, it is poorly understood. The standard definitions are simplistic and miss the essence of trust, which is highly changeable and sometimes fragile.

- Trust indicates a willingness to become vulnerable to another based on confident, positive expectations of his/her conduct.
- Trust is a psychological state comprising the intention to accept vulnerability based upon positive expectations of the intentions or behavior of another.
- Trust is an individual's belief in and willingness to act on the basis of the words, actions, and decisions of another.

Trust between people reflects a range of variables at a particular moment. We believe that trust should be viewed as a relationship-investment account. The balance can build over time, either incrementally through small contributions or substantially through larger deposits. Conversely, it can be decreased—even depleted—through actions that damage or destroy trust. Understanding how trust works is critical to avoiding inadvertent reductions to the account.

Trust is the foundation of successful procurement. The speed with which layered strategies can be implemented is largely governed by the degree of trust between stakeholders and Procurement. In short, an open, trusting relationship between stakeholders and Procurement provides the foundation for potential change; both parties are open to new ideas and are confident that the other party's interests and vision are aligned with their own. Trust is an amorphous topic. Below is a model to help you understand how trust is established and expanded.

Topic-Specific Nomenclature

As in most industries, procurement professionals use a range of terminology with specific definitions. The following terms and definitions are used in this section:

- ***None.***

The Tool: The Gaire/Stavrand Trust Model[1]

Our model is based on the typical dynamic where one party is the "trust builder" or "trust initiator," and the other party is the "trust target." We express our model as follows:

Trust Indicator = (*Individual History* + *Situational Dynamics* + *Rapport* + *Competence*) x *Integrity*

The format is intentionally mathematical. Here is an explanation: Each element has value on its own; the first four elements are added together, then multiplied by integrity. The result of the integrity factor will either cause a substantive increase in the "trust account" or a reduction in or cancellation of the account.

The term *trust indicator* is used to describe the predicted/expected environment for a trusting relationship to develop, based on analysis of the variables. The *trust indicator* represents a point in time; the analysis provides the basis for further, positive activities to build the relationship.

The Tool: Understanding and Building Trust in the Real World

1. Individual History

We all know people who have trusted someone and had the relationship work out poorly. We also know people whose trust has led to positive outcomes. A relationship can be personal, familial, or professional. What matters are the outcome and how the person perceived the breach or fulfillment of trust. Someone

1. Developed by Susan Gaire, MD FACOG (retired), and Erik Stavrand, SPHR, CPSM, PCC

who was in a relationship in which trust was breached may be wary of trusting again and magnify the seriousness of past betrayals. Conversely, individuals with a history of positive experiences will bring this to new relationships. Each person has a unique history of personal and professional relationships based on trust. The results of these experiences and the way an individual positions them in his/her value scheme predetermine how willing he/she will be to form new trust-based relationships.

We advocate approaching each "trust target" with an open mind and seeking to understand that person's background. Open-ended dialogue facilitates an exchange of the most relevant and easily shared experiences.

Trust Indicator = (Individual History + *Situational Dynamics* + *Rapport* + *Competence*) x *Integrity*

Individual History of the Trust Target

5 - Flawless history; very open and receptive
4 - Cautious optimism
3 - Neutral; "show me"
2 - Unhealthy skepticism
1 - Negative history; damaged and self-protective

Variable scoring: A history of positive experiences makes it more likely that a person will develop openness to new opportunities. With substantial effort, a highly negative history may be ameliorated to create neutrality or cautious optimism. A negative history is difficult to overcome and will require many "investments" before any appreciable change in overall trust is noticed.

Perspective	History
Trust Target	• Is this person going to hurt me? • Is this person going to help me?
Trust Builder	• Where is this person coming from? • If he/she seems skeptical or cautious, why? • What were his/her past experiences? • If he/she is immediately positive, how can I build on his/her history and take it to the next level?

* * *

2. Situational Dynamics

In many instances, we have no choice but to trust, at least initially, those who become part of our situation or circumstances. Think of the severely injured driver of a car who comes under the care of a first responder. The natural response under these circumstances is to appreciate and value the support of the new person as he/she assesses vital signs and conducts other appropriate interventions. Imagine, however, if someone is stopped at a traffic light and the same person, absent any uniform or identification, asks the driver to step out of the car to perform an "assessment." In the second case, the situational need to trust this person is low—virtually zero—and the driver's openness is appropriately reduced.

Responses boil down to this question: How urgently does the trust target perceive the need for the offering? The answer can range from an acute desire for some modification to acceptance of the status quo with no reason to alter current practices.

It is worth emphasizing that it is the trust target who must judge whether or not the current situation is acceptable. As long as he/she perceives that no change is required, he/she will not trust someone who is advocating change.

Trust Indicator = (*Individual History* + Situational Dynamics + *Rapport* + *Competence*) x *Integrity*

Situational Dynamics

5 - Instant action required
4 - Near-term action preferred
3 - Neutral
2 - Little to no pressure for change
1 - Deep satisfaction with current arrangements

Variable scoring: A person with acute needs will openly welcome help (subject to the other variables). A person who is satisfied with a damaging/detrimental situation would benefit from information that helps him/her see its potential consequences (e.g., a stakeholder who has been using the same supplier for ten-plus years with no market engagement may not realize that the supply market has continued to evolve and improve and that he/she has been left behind).

Note: Of the various elements of the model, this is the one variable where we all naturally keep our antenna tuned for fraud; "Everything is fine; why do I need your help?"

Perspective	Situation
Trust Target	• Do I need help? • How much and how quickly?
Trust Builder	• Does the other party need help? • Does the other party know it? • Why do he/she need help? • How much and how quickly?

* * *

3. Rapport

Personal rapport is often thought to be a proxy for trust. ("He seems very nice and likable, so I trust him.") This is, however, not a sufficient reason and may, in some cases, be irrelevant. From "natural salesmen," who are gregarious and outgoing, to quiet introverts and those with abrasive personalities, people have their own interactive styles. Personal styles and varied situations determine how quickly and how well rapport is established.

Trust Indicator = (*Individual History* + *Situational Dynamics* + Rapport + *Competence*) x *Integrity*

Rapport / Style of the Trust Builder

5 - Engaging; gregarious
4 - Affable; polite
3 - Neutral; polite
2 - Distant; reserved
1 - Difficult; prickly

Variable scoring: Rapport is either present or absent in a new relationship. You may naturally "click" with certain people, yet may not immediately relate to others. The test is whether positive rapport can be created. This can be directly between individuals or augmented by the referral from a trusted third party who can lend his/her relationship to the situation. Critical situations can still proceed in the absence of rapport if the other variables are strong enough to carry the situation.

Perspective	Rapport
Trust Target	• Does this person's style motivate me to engage or avoid?
Trust Builder	• Does my style build walls or break them down?

* * *

4. Competence

How competent you perceive a person to be directly affects whether or not you choose to trust that individual. In the prior example of a car accident, if the first responder were an EMT who was wearing a uniform and was able to calmly articulate how he/she could help the driver, the injured person would be inclined to trust him/her far more than she would a clearly agitated bystander who did not seem to know what he/she was doing.

All relationships are founded on competence in one way or another. People choose to associate with those who possess what they consider admirable, respected capabilities. Individuals who are recognized for their competence can accelerate the overall trust-building process.

Trust Indicator = (*Individual History + Situational Dynamics + Rapport +* Competence) x *Integrity*

Perceived/Demonstrated Competence of the Trust Builder

5 - World-class competence
4 - Local leader
3 - Average
2 - Slacker
1 - Known incompetent

Variable scoring: The absence of known competence will invariably lead to a "test" of the trust builder by the trust target. A positive result sets the stage for progress; a negative result will place extreme pressure on the other variables to carry the relationship. We can imagine a circumstance in which a fully competent individual is perceived as less than fully competent but is allowed to proceed, albeit with a watchful eye.

Perspective	Competence
Trust Target	• Does he/she know what he/she is doing? • Will he/she cause a bad outcome that affects me? • Will he/she cause a bad outcome that affects others to/for whom I am accountable?
Trust Builder	• How can I use my skills and knowledge in this situation to demonstrate my value to this person? • How can I prevent my gaps from showing?

* * *

5. Integrity

Integrity is the single most important variable in building a fully functioning relationship founded on trust. Individuals who are known to say one thing to one person and a different thing to someone else lack integrity; organizations or systems that enunciate clear goals and principles but tolerate or encourage conflicting behavior have low integrity. All parties in the trust-based relationship understand these dynamics and adjust their behavior accordingly. Conversely, individuals and organizations that consistently match word, deed, and intent demonstrate integrity.

We include the organizational dynamic in this section on integrity because the broader context is vitally important to any situation. Underpinning all individual relationships is the fabric of the organization within which the relationship exists. The clarity with which the organization's goals are stated and supported by real actions directly affects trust between individuals at lower levels. On one hand, this can result in positive relationship-building activities; on the other hand, it can have the opposite result—self-protection and reluctance to risk forming relationships. Many organizations suffer integrity lapses during periods of change and strife (not to excuse them but to point out reality), but it is never acceptable for people to compromise their integrity. This principle underlies all social norms: The sins of the organization do not excuse the sins of the individual.

Trust Indicator = (*Individual History + Situational Dynamics + Rapport + Competence*) x Integrity

Individual, Organizational, or Systemic Integrity

5 - Word is bond; quick and thorough follow-up
4 - Supportive but slow
3 - Neutral
2 - Retreating into history
1 - Broken; no follow-through; systems not linked

Variable scoring: The absence of integrity is a barrier to functional, trusting relationships. All other variables can be present (or perceived to be). However, if the integrity of the situation, organization, or trust builder (or, to turn the model around, the trust target) is missing, the relationship is doomed. Conversely, a positive, trusting relationship is rapidly built when integrity is obviously present.

Perspective	Integrity
Trust Target	• Do I have to work with this person? • Does he/she have to work with me? • What if we don't achieve results?
Trust Builder	• Are our goals aligned? • If so, how can I build on that? • If not, what can I do to build alignment? • Is it possible?

* * *

Calculating Your Totals

Once each parameter is assessed, an aggregate score can be calculated as follows:

Trust Indicator = (*Individual History* {1 – 5} + *Situational Dynamics* {1 – 5} + *Rapport* {1 – 5} + *Competence* {1 – 5}) x *Integrity* {1 – 5}

Trust Indicator	Interpretive comments
80 - 100	Exceptional basis for a deep, trusting relationship exists. Maintain a strong focus on continual openness to ensure that trust is not taken for granted.
60 - 80	There is a solid foundation for extending the relationship.
30 - 60	There is a weak foundation for the relationship. Engage in progressive trust-building exercises and an open dialogue to build the relationship.
0 - 30	There is a seriously compromised basis for a trusting relationship. Proceed slowly to more fully understand the situation and engage in targeted trust-building activities, using a mutually agreed-upon third party as appropriate.

Summary

Establishing and developing trust-based relationships is the foundation of world-class procurement. The topic is deeply personal—both for you and for the person with whom you are building trust. Keep an open mind, and listen for the obvious and subtle clues.

CPO Insights from Chris

As outlined earlier in this chapter, a leader's ability to build trust is dependent upon the quality of the results, both in terms of *what* is delivered and *how* it is delivered. In fact, it is often more about the *how* than the *what.* Trust is built on the professionalism of associates/team members who work in Procurement. We find that employees and leaders often underestimate the importance of the *how* when they are building relationships and focus solely on the numbers—the *what.* This is a classic example of how critical relationship skills are to delivering business results. This applies equally to internal stakeholders and external suppliers.

To be successful, you need to understand some of the factors that build trust within your organization. One of the most significant drivers is the culture.

- Is it combative or collaborative?
- Are there passive-aggressive behaviors on the part of management?
- How are employees rewarded?
- What behaviors are encouraged?
- How supportive of the procurement program is the CEO or board?
- What are the typical behavior styles of the employees with whom you engage?

Personal style and personality differences are vital factors in assigning employees to interact with stakeholders. There are many behavior models available. I have been successful using Myers-Briggs Type Indicator (MBTI®).

These are just a few conclusions from my own experiences that you should consider as you try to build a culture in which trust is the norm, not the exception. You can build trust, but it can easily be broken if members of your department do not continue to be aware of the *what* and *how* of their interactions with stakeholders. Invest in building your employees' capabilities and interpersonal skills. Do not fall into the trap of thinking that delivering the *what* alone will build trust and make you a valued partner of key stakeholders across the company; without stakeholder trust, you will fail.

TEMPLATE: Trust, page 1

Your Name:	Trust Target:
Trust Indicator = (*Individual History* {1 – 5} + *Situational Dynamics* {1 – 5} + *Rapport* {1 – 5} + *Competence* {1 – 5}) x *Integrity* {1 – 5}	

Trust Parameter	Scoring Criteria	Observable Behaviors, Perceptions, and Feedback	"As Is" Trust Score
Individual History	5 = Flawless history; very open and receptive 4 = Cautious optimism 3 = Neutral; *"show me"* 2 = Unhealthy skepticism 1 = Negative history; damaged and self-protective		
Situational Dynamics	5 = Instant action required 4 = Near-term action preferred 3 = Neutral 2 = Little to no pressure for change 1 = Deep satisfaction with current arrangements		
Rapport	5 = Engaging; gregarious 4 = Affable; polite 3 = Neutral; polite 2 = Distant; reserved 1 = Difficult; prickly		
Competence	5 = World-class competence 4 = Local leader 3 = Average 2 = Slacker 1 = Known incompetent		
Subtotal		Total the above scores	
Integrity	5 = Word is bond; quick and thorough follow-up 4 = Supportive but slow 3 = Neutral 2 = Retreating into history 1 = Broken; no follow-through; systems not linked		
Total		Multiply the subtotal scores by the Integrity score	

Trust Indicator	Interpretive Comments
80 - 100	Exceptional basis for a deep, trusting relationship exists. Maintain a strong focus on continual openness to ensure that trust is not taken for granted.
60 - 80	There is a solid foundation for extending the relationship.
30 - 60	There is a weak foundation for the relationship. Engage in progressive trust-building exercises and an open dialogue to build the relationship.
0 - 30	There is a seriously compromised basis for a trusting relationship. Proceed slowly to more fully understand the situation and engage in targeted trust-building activities, using a mutually agreed-upon third party as appropriate.

TEMPLATE: Trust, page 2

Your Name:	Trust Target:
Current Trust Score:	Trust Target's Role:

Trust Parameter	Trust-building Considerations	How will I build that person's trust in me?
Individual History	• Where is this person coming from?	
Situational Dynamics	• Does he/she need help? • Why? • How much and how quickly?	
Rapport	• Does my style build walls with others or break them down?	
Competence	• How can I use my skills in this space successfully? • How can I prevent my gaps from showing?	
Integrity	• Are our goals aligned? • If yes, how can I build on that? • If not, what can I do to build alignment? • Is it possible?	

20 Value Calculations and Governance

Topic Area Assessment Statements

Review these statements from your perspective as a procurement leader. If you "strongly agree" with all of the statements, you may wish to skip to the next topic. But, if you have some doubts about any of them, we recommend that you read this chapter and engage in some self-reflection.

- Procurement's measures of value contribution are linked to business priorities.
- Key stakeholders acknowledge that Procurement's value-contribution calculations are credible and "real."
- Procurement measures its own effectiveness (value contribution) and efficiency (resource utilization).

Topic Introduction: Value Calculations and Governance

> "If you're not keeping score, you're just practicing."
> —Jan Leschly, former CEO of GlaxoSmithKline (GSK) and professional tennis player

Measuring performance, a procurement requirement, is core to many aspects of business. Most procurement-transformation efforts are the result of difficult business conditions and the need to quickly achieve third-party cost savings and cash-flow improvements.

Measurement for the sake of measurement, however, is a waste of time and resources. Measurements must be:

1. Aligned with the overarching business strategy
2. Consistent with current business priorities
3. Vetted and approved by the appropriate business leaders
4. Comprehensive and reflective of the entire impact on the organization; not solely about cost, but also about effectiveness and efficiency
5. Collected consistently over time to assess the impact of strategic choices

While there are many books on the topic of measurement, the focus of this chapter is on the range of procurement-related measures that demonstrate the contribution Procurement makes to the broader organization.

Topic-Specific Nomenclature

As in most industries, procurement professionals use a range of terminology with specific definitions. The following terms and definitions are used in this section[1]:

- ***Return on Total Assets (ROTA)*** **–** A ratio that measures a company's earnings before interest and taxes (EBIT) against its total net assets; the ratio is considered an indicator of how effectively a company is using its assets to generate earnings before contractual obligations must be paid. To calculate: ROTA = EBIT/Total Net Assets where EBIT is Net Income + Interest Expense + Taxes.

- ***Return on Assets (ROA)*** **–** An indicator of how profitable a company is relative to its total assets; ROA provides a picture of how efficient management is at using its assets to generate earnings. Calculated by dividing a company's annual earnings by its total assets, ROA is displayed as a percentage. Sometimes, this is referred to as "return on investment." The formula for Return on Assets is: ROA = Net Income/Total Assets.

- ***Earnings Before Interest, Taxes, Depreciation, and Amortization (EBITDA)*** **–** Used to evaluate the financial health of a company

- ***Days Payable Outstanding (DPO)*** **–** How long it takes a company to pay its invoices from trade creditors, such as suppliers; the formula to calculate DPO = ending accounts payable (cost of sales/number of days).

- ***Vendor-Managed Inventory (VMI)*** **–** Inventory placed by a vendor at the buying company's location that is managed and typically financed by the vendor until it is consumed. This practice reduces capital employed by reducing the need to purchase inventory before it is consumed.

- ***Generally Accepted Accounting Principles (GAAP)*** **–** The common set of accounting principles, standards, and procedures that companies use to compile their financial statements; GAAP are a combination of authoritative standards (set by policy boards) and simply the commonly accepted ways of recording and reporting accounting information.

1. Financial definitions from investopedia.com.

The Tool: Value Calculations and Governance

It is important to think of value calculations and the related stakeholder governance as a continuous process. Many procurement leaders consider the process completed when the value calculations are first agreed upon with the stakeholders and then implemented. The reality, however, is that the stakeholder base is ever changing, and the business strategy is always evolving. Do not become complacent in this area. Additionally, focus on the "we" of delivery and rarely, if ever, proclaim results as a "procurement accomplishment." World-class procurement is a team sport, and the value calculations and governance work are best viewed as the rules of the game, with the associated scorekeeping process agreed to by all the participants.

Aligned with the overarching business strategy

Business strategies evolve over time and can be seen in the core measures used by the board of directors to assess the overall performance of a company. Commonly used measures include:

- Return on total assets (ROTA)
- Return on assets (ROA)
- Earnings before interest, taxes, depreciation, and amortization (EBITDA)

Each of these measures emphasizes a different financial choice (internal asset utilization versus external assets, income statement-based savings, etc.). The core procurement measure related to the business's strategy is invariably value delivery, which includes savings, cost avoidance, and functional operating cost (also known as the cost to procure).

Consistent with the current business priorities

In addition to the over-arching strategy drivers, you must also address near-term business priorities, which commonly include:

- Cash flow/days payable outstanding
- Capital employed/inventory turns
- Sales/profit at risk

Each of these measures highlights different choices within the supply chain:

- Cash-flow – accelerating or slowing the supplier-payment process
- Capital employed – vendor-management inventory, just-in-time deliveries, etc.
- Sales at risk – strategic risk (typically related to sole/single-sourced critical materials and services)

Vetted and approved by the applicable business leaders

Governance of the value contribution is a collaborative process that involves key stakeholders and the Finance Department. Simply put, value contribution is not real or valid unless or until it is vetted and approved. Until this process is complete, the value contribution is regarded as potential (at best) or false/not believable (at worst).

The procurement leader is responsible for pulling together the requisite financial leaders and key stakeholders, who will agree upon:

- The definitions of value
- The review and approval processes
- The budgetary implications for stakeholders

The key point for Procurement to remember is that value delivery is always a team sport; it can never be something that Procurement alone claims to have done for or to the stakeholders. It is always the stakeholders' spend that is involved, and their cooperation and collaboration cannot be compromised.

The entire process must be documented and periodically improved as the organization's needs evolve. *Note: This process requires regular training of Procurement staff, as well as stakeholders or Finance's staff. The normal turnover in an organization will render a large percentage of employees new to the definitions and review/approval process. Never assume that the process is fully understood and completely accepted.*

Typical value definitions

Price savings or increases in prices of the underlying commodity or service

- The new price paid is below the current or standard price. The price is less than previously paid for goods and services that fulfill a comparable business requirement in terms of quality and quantity; the price paid applies equally to goods and services.
- This is typically called a positive purchase-price variance (PPV). Standards are reset periodically (typically, as part of the annual budget process).
- Volume rebates are often credited to PPV and taken in the year they are received, per the generally accepted accounting principles (GAAP rules).
- *Note: Price savings is the most commonly used form of procurement-value contribution and is the easiest to support as valid. It often results in direct budget changes and, therefore, does have an impact on the bottom line—profit and loss (P&L)—which drives senior-executive (sponsor) alignment and support.*

Cost avoidance

- Negotiated price that is not lower than the previously paid price but avoids a price increase by eliminating the inflationary increase and keeping prices flat.

- *Note: Although avoiding price increases is a worthy goal, it is often viewed skeptically by stakeholders. Clearly, cost avoidance does not affect the P&L in the same way as a price decrease. Different forms of documentation are required (e.g., quotes to demonstrate the decrease from initial offer to final offer). In high-inflation economies (e.g., Argentina in the 2010s), the task of keeping prices flat was (and remains) an ambitious goal; price reductions are extraordinary and rare.*

Capital cost reductions or increases

- Capital projects are typically nonrecurring and often cannot be measured using price decreases. To the extent possible, segregate the project elements; identify the recurring elements for direct year-to-year or project-to-project comparisons (e.g., general-contractor time at the various levels); and review the balance using cost-avoidance methodology.

- *Note: There are many potential value levers in the capital budget, such as demand/specification management, proactive strategy development that covers recurring spend elements, or moving the bid-and-buy activity to a lower-cost environment. The value delivery here is real, but is only appreciated if Procurement is seen as producing results and not wasting time by engaging in protracted bidding when suppliers have already been selected.*

Definitions and reporting periods for savings types

- One-off savings (increases) – Savings that will not result in a benefit for more than twelve months; reported in the year the goods or services are received.

- Ongoing savings (increases) – Savings underpinned by existing pricing agreements whose terms extend beyond twelve months. These savings will reduce the level of annual spend beyond twelve months. The baseline is reset at the end of twelve months; only incremental savings or increases will be measured through the term of the contract.

Other considerations

- Increasing payment terms (paying suppliers more slowly) positively affects organizational cash flow and may generate measurable value. This depends on the organizational strategy and cost of capital.
- Eliminating penalties is a value that will be viewed in different ways by different organizations; some view this as price savings and others as a cost avoidance. This is best addressed during the value-governance planning process.
- Total cost savings that reflect changes across a supply chain are very important. These savings may be positive at the same time item price changes are negative. This is not uncommon. It is vital, however, for the concept of total cost to be well understood and accepted and for all of the associated savings claims to be absolutely verifiable. Often, an area of business is outsourced in the pursuit of lower total costs. The verification of results must extend to a person-by-person review of the before-and-after costs to ensure that they are valid. In addition, the governance process must include HR to ensure that all people-related considerations and calculations are consistent with the company practices and prevailing laws.
- Consider exchange-rate effects to be certain that all calculations are consistent with the estimated value and impact of world currencies.

Typical Value Review-and-Approval Process Steps

1. Submissions above the tracking/approval threshold (typically, $25K per year) are entered into the tracking system as "pending review" by a sourcing professional.
2. The "pending-review" submissions (including backup documentation) are reviewed by procurement management, revised as needed, and forwarded to Finance and stakeholders.
3. Finance and stakeholders review the submission, request additional information if necessary, and approve or disapprove as appropriate.
4. The actual value delivery versus the estimated value is measured. Interventions occur as needed.
5. The aggregate results are shared with the collaborative governance body to provide information for current and future plans.

Anticipated supply-base-linked savings are often reflected in changed budgets—commonly called a "target bake-in process." This resetting of budgets must be openly addressed during the process of establishing budgets and strategies. *If "procurement savings" result in stakeholder budget cuts without input and approval from stakeholders, they will not recur, and Procurement's success will be short-lived.*

Summary

Results matter. Be sure that your organization is tracking the results that are directly linked to the broader organizational strategy and recognized as valid and legitimate by stakeholders. Establishing an ongoing measurement scheme and governance is a core element of collaborative-spend governance and integral to building trust with the stakeholder community.

CPO Insights from Chris

Trust is built with the business community when it believes you are delivering value. Many of us have heard from our stakeholders, "I do not see the money or the benefit that you are promising." Agreeing on the formulas you will use to track value is important, but then, stakeholders must vet the savings and agree that they are (1) real and (2) of the size described by Procurement.

The role of Finance is key; Finance should be seen as the keeper of the keys when it comes to the benefits Procurement will deliver. This is not Procurement's money; it is the company's money. As a rule, when you start a project, identify a member of Finance and a customer to work with you on the approval of the benefit (i.e., the stakeholders must agree that the decrease in prices [or increase in prices but with a longer useful life] is real and valuable to them). Once a benefit is approved, have a Finance employee audit the results so that the business realizes the benefit. This builds credibility with senior executives. The benefit's value should be reviewed quarterly with your executive council. We also suggest tracking the benefits back to business budgets.

1. The 'Gold Standard' benchmark for the Cost-to-Procurement benchmark is the *Hackett Group's Book of Numbers*. It is available for a wide range of industries on a global basis and is very comprehensive.

21 Competence Assessment

Topic Area Assessment Statements

Review these statements from your perspective as a procurement leader. If you "strongly agree" with all of the statements, you may wish to skip to the next topic. But, if you have some doubts about any of them, we recommend that you read this chapter and engage in some self-reflection.

- My team and I know the team's professional strengths and weaknesses.
- My team and I have personal development plans and continuously seek to improve our capabilities and performance.
- My team and I are able to learn from others.
- My team and I select new team members to balance our current strengths and abilities.
- My team and I know our organization's strengths and weaknesses.
- My team and I have a plan to address the weaknesses of our team and maximize our collective strengths.

Topic Introduction: Self-Assessment and Development

Every leader brings a unique set of skills, abilities, and experiences to his/her current role. There is rarely a perfect fit between these attributes and the role. The role's needs are never constant, and requirements are ever changing. Leaders must continually evolve to meet the needs of the broader organization and to ensure their relevance.

The process of self-assessment requires a high level of self-awareness and an ability to objectively assess personal capabilities versus objective requirements of the role. This raises two fundamental questions:

1. Can you objectively assess your own strengths and weaknesses as a leader and as a procurement professional?
2. Do you know the current capability standards required in your present role? In the next role to which you aspire?

Objective self-assessment is difficult. Compare your abilities to known leaders in the field. How do you compare? What capabilities will you need in the future? Will you be ready? These are the essential questions you must answer in order to remain relevant to the company and successful as a leader.

Topic-Specific Nomenclature

As in most industries, procurement professionals use a range of terminology with specific definitions. The following terms and definitions are used in this section:

- ***Competence*** – The ability of an individual to properly fulfill the requirements of a task or position. A competency is a set of defined behaviors or attributes that provides a structured guide enabling the identification, evaluation, and development of individual employees.

The Tool: Competence Assessments

Competence assessment can be a very scary process; nobody wants to be viewed as incompetent. Competence assessment must, however, be a high-integrity process based on objective standards. Such an assessment is the basis for all development planning at the individual and organizational levels. Our experience in this area leads us to strongly recommend the following practices:

- Include all levels of Procurement in the assessment, including leaders.
- Use a third party to conduct thorough, objective evaluations.
- Only use the assessment results as a data source for *development plans.* Do not use the assessment process to identify and remove employees. (Use the balance of the HR processes to address poor performers.)

Self-Assessment as a Leader

There are many books on leadership and a number of instruments to assess personal leadership capabilities. The following are core elements of leadership for procurement leaders to consider:

Analytical ability

- Understand the current organizational situation.
- Develop plans to meet evolving needs.
- Measure plan success and develop effective problem-solving or remediation plans, activities, and actions.

Communication skills

- Write a clear and compelling plan (using all current tools).
- Verbally convey the plan to the appropriate audiences.

Self-discipline

- Focus on key priorities, and avoid unnecessary distractions.

Empathy

- Hear and appreciate different points of view (and cultures); understand and relate to them in a way that builds trust and a more successful plan.

Self-Assessment as a Procurement Leader

In addition to the generic elements of leadership, there are a number of critical strengths and abilities procurement leaders should possess. These are covered in detail in the area assessment sections in each chapter of this book. They can, however, be summarized in the following broad areas:

1. **Value Proposition** – The ability to develop a functional value proposition that meets the current and evolving needs of the broader organization
2. **Functional Strategy** – The ability to develop a functional strategy that links the company's needs with the supply base's capabilities in a way that assures appropriate strategic advantages, while balancing the organization's cost and value requirements
3. **Stakeholder Engagement** – The ability to understand and evaluate stakeholder communities in order to proactively engage them to build support
4. **Organizational Design and Deployment** – The ability to structure Procurement to achieve effectiveness, while efficiently stewarding the organization's resources
5. **Communications** – The ability to articulate the functional strategy and value proposition inside and outside of Procurement in a way that is clear and compelling to the respective stakeholder communities in the following way:
    - Inside the company but outside Procurement
    - Inside Procurement
    - Outside the company to suppliers
    - Outside the company to other key stakeholders (governments, NGOs, the press, etc.)

Once your self-assessment is complete, you should augment it with outside input. This can take the form of subordinate, peer, and manager feedback (360-degree feedback) or an external competence assessment. Regardless of the approach, it must be rigorous and valid; do not settle for "soft" feedback. After you receive this feedback, it is up to you to act on it and continue to develop yourself. Do not become lost in improvement tasks ("paralysis by analysis"). Pick one task; and focus your efforts there, while, at the same time, maintaining your strengths. Keep in mind the many reasons you are a successful leader.

Assessing the Procurement Function: A Competence Assessment Road Map

As the procurement leader, it is incumbent upon you to know the current competence of the department and to develop and implement a plan that matches its future competence to meet the business's needs. Many procurement leaders conduct this assessment themselves, but we recommend objective, third-party assessments. Developing a comprehensive, agreed-upon assessment and sharing it with senior leaders and HR is vital to building support for a transformation program.

A note on assessments: The word "assessment" is value-laden and strikes fear into some people, while having no effect on others. It is important to confirm and reiterate that the goal of assessment is to accelerate focused development, not to make retention/exit ("hire/fire") decisions. Embed this clear, yet principled message in all communications inside and outside of Procurement. We neither believe in nor advocate the use of a relatively brief capability "assessment" for employee-retention purposes. If the goal of the exercise is to change the size of an organization or the composition of the workforce, then the project must fully involve HR from all of the included geographies. The integrity of the process (or lack thereof) will be felt for years to come. Therefore, demonstrate high integrity, and get the process right the first time.

Step 1 – Identify the assessment scope and plan.

Once you decide to assess the procurement organization, start by assembling a core team, which should comprise procurement leaders, HR staff members, and outside experts.

The team must agree on the scope of the assessment across the following possible procurement activities:

- Centralized sourcing
- Decentralized sourcing
- Local buying/planning
- Shared services/outsourced staff
- Functional leadership

Many organizations have "shadow procurement" functions that are embedded in various departments of the company (particularly Marketing, Legal, and R&D). Should these functions be included in the core planning team? If you decide to include them, have the appropriate stakeholder leaders become part of the team.

Be certain that you have adequate staff available to plan and execute the entire assessment process. Assessing only a handful of employees at one or two sites is a fairly straightforward event, but when many employees across multiple sites are included in an assessment, it becomes vastly more complicated and requires rigorous planning and communications.

Step 2 – Establish the overarching procurement competence and level of requirements.

The starting points for the assessment process are Procurement's vision, future value proposition, and functional strategy, which include the following:

1) Required Procurement performance levels and timing
   a) What is Procurement expected to do now in the commercial relationship with suppliers and the company, and how will those expectations change in the future?
   b) What are non-procurement employees allowed to purchase (or commit to purchasing on an ongoing basis) without Procurement's support?
   c) How will their procurement performance be evaluated and improved over time?
   d) How will *this* situation change in the future?

2) Future role of the external supply chain
   a) Is the engagement of external suppliers increasing? Decreasing?
   b) Will supplier-based innovation be a key factor in the future?
   c) Based on any changes in the scope of future activity, will additional resources be required?
   d) Will resources with substantially different skill sets be required?
   e) Which current stakeholders will continue to be involved in commercial decision making?
   f) Which new stakeholders will participate?
3) Current and future role of functional leadership:
   a) Do procurement leaders currently lead their teams effectively?
   b) Do they participate productively as members of other leadership teams?
   c) Will these expectations change over time?
4) Current stakeholder perceptions and overall spend-governance model:
   a) How do key stakeholders and opinion leaders currently view Procurement?
   b) Is Procurement actively involved from the outset in the specification, supply market, and supplier decision-making process?
   c) If not, what is being done to address these issues and, if so, how firmly established is Procurement's involvement?

The answers to these questions create a comprehensive picture of the future of Procurement—both inside and outside of the department. The future view of capabilities and organization sizing should be tested across the appropriate leadership team to ensure alignment with existing and evolving business strategies.

Typical elements include the following headings and are then further divided into discrete sub-elements:

- Category and market expertise
- Procurement processes and tools (sourcing, supplier management, Six Sigma, etc.)
- Procurement "basics"—contracting, cost modeling, negotiations
- Stakeholder engagement
- Cross-functional team leadership

Note: For leaders, there is also a focus on leadership, coaching, and change planning.

Detailed Procurement Competencies

The following pages contain a range of procurement competencies. Your organization may use some of these or add to this list. These are included as a model to build on and modify for your use.

Procurement Competencies

The following three pages contain a comprehensive listing of typical procurement competencies and their descriptions.

Parameter	Skill set	Description
Interpersonal Skills	Collaboration/networking/teamwork	Knows who to work and consult with and when and how to do so
	Influencing skills	Persuades and influences others
	Communication skills	Relates well to all stakeholders at different levels
	Political awareness	Understands business situations and acts appropriately
	Conflict resolution	Defuses and solves conflicts
	Sensitivity to diverse cultures	Understands cultural sensitivities and diversity in conducting business
	Profile management	Able to project a positive personal as well as business image
Leading	Ambition and high aspirations	Sets high targets/goals and works to exceed them
	Inspirational/motivational skills	Fosters a willingness to challenge the status quo; sets a personal example of high standards, which inspires others
	Facilitation skills	Brings out the best in cross-functional teams; guides cross-functional teams toward high-quality results through application of sound processes
	Leadership ability	Builds and develops successful functional and cross-functional teams
	Coaching skills	Recognizes and mentors people
	Change management experience	Understands and has experience in all the dynamics of change
Individual Attributes	Appropriate values	Operates in an appropriate manner
	Ethics and personal integrity	Demonstrates integrity and ethical standards that are beyond reproach
	Energy/resilience/self-starter	Uses initiative, withstands pressure, and exhibits high energy
	Independent thinker	Challenges the status quo where appropriate
	Problem solver	Interprets and understands problems and solves them
	Conceptual thinker	Applies experiential, conceptual, and innovative thinking

Parameter	Skill set	Description
Category Management	Industry and category expertise	Possesses clear knowledge of the industry and category dynamics
	Fluency in category-management process	Has knowledge of the entire process and the tools and methods of applying them where they are appropriate
	Knowledge of best practice and benchmarking; external awareness	Understands the importance of benchmarking and best practice
	Source-plan creation and management	Competent at value delivery and ongoing management of source plan
	Risk management/business continuity	Keeps risk minimized and protection maximized
	Understanding of value add (value streams)	Understands the relationships in the value chains
Procurement Skills	Cost modeling (cost to produce the product or service)	Understands and fully utilizes cost modeling where appropriate
	Strategic negotiation	Knows how and when to engage suppliers
	Legal and contractual	Possesses knowledge of legal and contract law
	Dispute resolution	Defuses and solves disputes
	Commodities	Understands commodity trading and purchasing
	Capital projects	Has expertise in capital sourcing
	Low-cost region sourcing	Demonstrates expertise in low-cost country sourcing
	Supply-market analysis	Analyzes supply markets well
Supplier Management	Supplier assessment	Conducts technical and commercial appraisal of potential and existing sources of supply
	New-product sourcing	Has expertise in the new-product sourcing area
	Supplier performance management	Understands and manages suppliers' capabilities
	Service-level agreement (SLA) development and execution	Builds comprehensive SLAs for suppliers
	Supplier performance	Pursues supplier fulfillment of business requirements and contractual obligations

Parameter	Skill set	Description
Technology	E-business	Uses e-tools and specifically possesses e-auction expertise
	Systems knowledge	Understands the business systems utilized in the company and, as appropriate, by suppliers (e.g., electronic and just In time (JIT) ordering)
Stakeholder Management	Reporting	Knows how to measure and report in line with business needs
	Communication	Understands the role of communication, and possesses the skills to communicate effectively at all stakeholder levels
	Understanding of end-customer relationships	Understands who stakeholders are and what their needs are
	Internal – external management	Manages both internal and external stakeholders
	Profile management	Projects a positive personal as well as professional image of the business
Specific Company/ Market Knowledge	Knowledge of the company (and divisions as applicable)	Understands the company's history, operations, strategy, and drivers
	Business and strategy alignment	Understands the alignment of purchasing and business strategy
	New-product development process	Understands the business's new-product development process
	Competitor awareness/analysis	Identifies and analyzes business competitors
	Make versus buy	Strategically and operationally assesses the outsource/in source equation
General Business Skills	Management and supervisory skills	Knows how to deliver results to the company through effective management
	General commercial skill	Understands the marketing mix and what adds value to the company
	Significant contribution to business strategy	Is a quantifiable asset to the business
	Financial skills and measurement management	Understands and evaluates financial information
	Systems literacy	Understands the value and applicability of technology solutions
	Change/continuous improvement	Understands all the dynamics of change
	Project management	Delivers projects on time and on budget, using recognized project-management tools and processes

Each of the elements and sub-elements requires a rating scale. Rating-scale development is the subject of intense debate in the industry, with some favoring odd-numbered schemes (i.e., 1 to 3 or 1 to 5) and others preferring even numbers. Whatever your preference, pick one, and fully describe what the competency would look like in tangible terms for each sub-element and each rating. This is detailed work, but this detail will enable you to clarify each employee's role and create an effective development plan for that person.

The competence assessment scale must be consistent with the organization's values and practices and agreed upon by top management and HR. Below are two scoring options we have used in different situations; they are neither right nor wrong but reflect the organizations being assessed.

Option 1 – 5 Assessment Scoring Levels

Aware	Developing	Leader	Expert	Master
Knows about the topic; no demonstrated capability	Uses basic concepts, often with support	Is able to use the concepts/tools to deliver results	Leads others in applying the concepts/tools	Can teach the concepts/tools from a position of deep personal experience

Option 2 – 6 Assessment Scoring Levels

1	2	3	4	5	6
Has basic knowledge of the skill(s); is not yet applying the skill(s) with any real degree of fluency or expertise; and/or has not demonstrated application		Has working knowledge of the skill(s) and of their significance; uses the skill(s) at a basic or competent level to carry out his/her (if this in an individual) work; and is able to provide relevant illustrations of the applicability of the skill(s) to his/her work		Has an emerging or developed knowledge of the significance of the skill(s); is applying the skill(s) expertly and routinely to influence the quality of his/her work; and is able to provide quantifiable, substantive examples of the application of the skill(s)	

Once you develop the ratings, the next step is to determine the benchmark level of performance for each role you are assessing. A leader is clearly expected to have broad stakeholder engagement and management capabilities, while a sourcing manager (whether inside or outside of Procurement) will be expected to have current, in-depth category and market expertise.

Determining the expected competency benchmarks is a core activity for the procurement leadership team (with appropriate HR support). Outside input can be useful, but the decision on required competency levels is ultimately up to the leadership team.

The following pages contain a sample template for documenting competency level benchmarks across typical procurement roles.

Step 3 – Identify the assessment candidates.
Assessments will take multiple forms, depending on an employee's role. The table below outlines the various scenarios:

<table>
<tr><th>Role</th><th>Method of Assessment</th></tr>
<tr><td>Analyst</td><td rowspan="3">• Online self-assessment
• In-person comprehensive assessment versus assessment of competence elements and benchmark performance</td></tr>
<tr><td>Buyer</td></tr>
<tr><td>Sourcing manager</td></tr>
<tr><td>Manager/director</td><td rowspan="2">• Online self-assessment
• In-person comprehensive assessment versus assessment of competence elements (including leadership and organizational-change elements) and benchmark performance</td></tr>
<tr><td>Vice president/unit or function leader</td></tr>
</table>

Based on this table, a comprehensive table of assessment candidates should be created, reviewed, and prioritized with the implementation leadership team. Once the team agrees on the path forward, begin notifying employees and conducting assessments.

Step 4 – Plan for and conduct the assessments.
Each affected individual must understand the process, purpose, and outcomes of assessment. The communications processes must be thorough, slightly repetitive, and in multimedia formats (e.g., in writing, on the company's intranet, video, etc.) to ensure comprehension.

Online assessments (both in the form of self-assessments and stand-alone assessments for stakeholders) may be performed at the employee's workplace or any other computer he/she chooses, as long as privacy is assured.

The assessment interviews, however, must be conducted in a private setting, such as a conference room or an office with a door. Ensure confidentiality. The goal is for the employee to share his/her relevant experiences and *fully describe his/her capability to perform the task* in a conversational/informal setting. Local HR staff members may attend as part of the planning process. Plan on two hours per interview, with ninety minutes of dialogue and thirty minutes for the interviewer to document the conversation. *Note: If an interviewer is conducting multiple assessments per day, he/she must fully document each session before proceeding with the next one. It is too easy to blur the results from one participant to the next.*

Prework

Prior to the interview, each participant submits prework, including the following information:

- Name
- Current role
- Length of time in current role
- Company name
- Line manager's name
- Work history (including any significant roles prior to joining the current company)
- Educational background since leaving school
- Professional training
- Additional information

The assessment interview

Each interview is conducted separately in a private room; the average length of the interview is an hour and a half. The flow of conversation follows the information submitted by the individual, including his/her relevant work history and answers to the required questions. At the conclusion of each interview, the participant is briefed on when to expect feedback. He/she is given the interviewer's business card and invited to share any additional information he/she wishes to share.

Data collection

At the conclusion of the interview, the interviewer will document his/her assessment of the employee and make a note of development options he/she suggests.

Note: Each interview is intended to be thorough and engaging but cannot (and is not intended to) supplant years of management assessments and related development activities. Each draft report must be reviewed with the appropriate procurement leader(s) before it is completed to be certain that nothing important has inadvertently been omitted.

Step 5 – Document the findings in individual and group reports.

At the end of the assessment process, each employee will receive a personalized development plan, which will include a report containing both qualitative feedback (potential development actions) and quantitative feedback (his/her own and others' assessments as they relate to benchmark expectations).

In addition to individual reports, prepare one for each "natural" workgroup. This report should contain individual, as well as aggregate quantitative and qualitative results.

Recommended report format

Quantitative feedback includes:

- Benchmark ratings
- External assessment of the individual
- Individual's self-reported assessment collected via an online survey tool
- Composite graph of all of the above

Qualitative feedback includes any relevant findings from the interview process and related development options.

Step 6 – Review the overall findings with leadership and develop phased plans.

The assessment process will yield a number of common and/or high-priority themes. It is important to the overall process, as well as the company's acceptance of the process, to establish a list of previously agreed-upon development suggestions. These might include core courses (conducted internally or outside of the organization), development rotations, mentoring assignments, or other credible and sustainable options.

Step 7 – Review the reports with leaders, and distribute to employees.

The employee's manager should review every report before it is finalized to be sure that it is fair and complete. Then, the employee and his/her manager should discuss the report, in person. The goal is to increase individual and organizational capability in order to meet business needs. By the end of the review, the outcome should be a mutually approved and documented in a development plan. Finally, all of the agreed-upon development actions from Step 1 and beyond should be incorporated into the employee's and his/her manager's performance goals to encourage the employee's focus and ongoing efforts.

The Feedback Process

Procurement Leadership

Draft Reports – Each draft report (with the exception of the employee's own report) is reviewed in draft form with the appropriate procurement leader prior to finalization to ensure completeness and accuracy (not to shape or influence the findings).

Finalized Reports – Each final report is reviewed in person with the CPO and appropriate Procurement leadership team members to discuss any additional thoughts, as well as the recommended development plan. The overall team findings are reviewed with the CPO as well. Include the appropriate HR participation in both reviews.

Individual

Procurement leader reviews the assessment report with the individual and any intermediary managers. *Note: We do not believe it is appropriate for an external assessing organization to review the findings with the interviewee. Leaders within the company are the most appropriate people to handle this; they must own and support the results.*

The findings are reviewed, and the individual and his/her procurement leader resolve any disagreements and finalize a development plan. It is up to the responsible procurement leader to create a supportive environment for agreement and execution of the plan.

The individual employee is then responsible for completing development activities and modifying his/her ongoing work methods as necessary.

Summary

Competence assessments should be one of Procurement's ongoing priorities. Procurement transformation, while partially an online process, is fundamentally a people-based event. It is up to you to continuously broaden Procurement's individual and group capabilities. By doing so, you will be able to engage stakeholders, think strategically, drive supplier improvements, and deliver ever-improving results. Keep the competence results in front of leaders and employees; they are both responsible for continuous improvement.

CPO Insights from Chris

Building and assessing talent are perennial topics for procurement leaders. Expectations and the talent required to meet those expectations change from year to year. In order to calibrate and align expectations, you will have to meet with employees regularly. Being overly critical of an employee's abilities may adversely affect his/her performance and morale. To have any long-term impact, your discussions must include clear examples.

As you look at competence, it is critical to have a baseline for what you are looking for—something that is hard to set internally. Leaders often inflate an employee's competence, which may lead to inflating that person's self-perception as well.

I strongly recommend calling on the support of a strong HR department (or third party) to facilitate the assessment process versus bringing in a third-party assessment company. It is simply too easy to stay internally focused and convince yourself that the development is more complete than it really is. There is no perfect solution here; as it is, conducting an assessment is a mix of emotion and facts. Feedback should be a gift, but it is not always seen as one. Creating an environment in which employees see the openness around the assessment, rather than as a basis of retention, helps build a degree of trust. Conducting assessments is not a comfortable process for the employee or the manager, but it is a necessary one.

TEMPLATE: Establishing Benchmark Competency Levels Across Typical Procurement Roles, page 1

Parameter/Skill set		Functional Role					
		Analyst	**Buyer**	**Sourcing manager**	**Sourcing director**	**Area vice president**	**CPO**
Interpersonal Skills	Collaborating/networking/ team-working						
	Influencing skills						
	Communication skills						
	Political awareness						
	Conflict resolution						
	Sensitivity to diverse cultures						
	Profile management						
Leading	Ambition and high aspirations						
	Inspirational/motivational skills						
	Facilitation skill						
	Leadership ability						
	Coaching skills						
	Change management experience						
Individual Attributes	Appropriate values						
	Ethics and personal integrity						
	Energy/resilience/self-starter						
	Independent thinker						
	Problem solver						
	Conceptual thinker						

TEMPLATE: Establishing Benchmark Competency Levels Across Typical Procurement Roles, page 2

Parameter / Skill set		Functional Role					
		Analyst	Buyer	Sourcing manager	Sourcing director	Area vice president	CPO
Category Management	Industry and category expertise						
	Fluency in category-management process						
	Knowledge of best practice/ benchmarking/external awareness						
	Source plan creation and management						
	Risk management/business continuity						
	Understanding of value add (value streams)						
Procurement Skills	Cost modeling (cost to produce the product or service)						
	Strategic negotiation						
	Legal and contractual						
	Dispute resolution						
	Commodity						
	Capital projects						
	LCR sourcing						
	Supply-market analysis						
Supplier Management	Supplier assessment						
	New-product sourcing						
	Supplier-performance management						
	Service-level agreement construction						
	Supplier performance						

TEMPLATE: Establishing Benchmark Competency Levels Across Typical Procurement Roles, page 3

Parameter/Skill set		Functional Role					
		Analyst	Buyer	Sourcing manager	Sourcing director	Area vice president	CPO
Technology	E-business						
	Systems knowledge						
Stakeholder Management	Reporting						
	Communication						
	End-customer relationship understanding						
	Internal-external management						
	Profile management						
Specific Company / Market Knowledge	Knowledge of the company (and divisions as applicable)						
	Business and strategy alignment						
	New product development process						
	Competitor awareness/ analysis						
	Make versus buy						
General Business Skills	Management and supervisory skills						
	General commercial skill						
	Significant contribution to business strategy						
	Financial skills, measurement management						
	Systems literacy						
	Change/continuous improvement						
	Project management						

22 Procurement Organizational Design

Topic Area Assessment Statements

Review these statements from your perspective as a procurement leader. If you "strongly agree" with all of the statements, you may wish to skip to the next topic. But, if you have some doubts about any of them, we recommend that you read this chapter and engage in some self-reflection.

- Procurement's organizational design ensures optimum functional efficiency and effectiveness.
- Procurement employees understand the rationale behind the organizational design.
- The leadership structure is lean and efficient and provides development opportunities for future leaders.

Topic Introduction: Procurement Organizational Design

The design of any organization is a complex, nuanced endeavor. The approach that follows is a distillation of the topic and is not intended to provide the only template for this process. Rather, it is intended to help procurement leaders frame the task and engage stakeholders appropriately.

Every procurement function must perform its organizational mission (measured by effectiveness) within the constraints of allocated resources (measured by efficiency). These measures must also reflect continuous improvement.[1]

Key choices in the design of the procurement function include:

- Degree of centralization based on whether the business is managed by corporate, by region, or by business units on discrete P&Ls
- Processes that typically include requisition to payment, although accounts payable may be retained by Finance
- Alignment of core strategic categories with corresponding stakeholder communities

1. Effectiveness is typically measured as "Value Delivered" and Efficiency as the "Cost-to-Procure" (functional costs as either a percentage of sales or the respective spend). Hackett Consulting publishes and charges for the currently recommended benchmark for these measures.

- Procurement organization's maturity and capabilities (i.e., nascent organizations are inherently less capable than well-established, sophisticated organizations)
- Procurement's or the business's acceptance of outsourcing

None of these are simple, yes-or-no choices; they are all subtly different. Understanding these nuances is the key to success of current and evolving organizational designs.

Topic-Specific Nomenclature

As in most industries, procurement professionals use a range of terminology with specific definitions. The following terms and definitions are used in this section:

- ***None.***

The Tool: Procurement Organizational Design

The intent of this tool is to provide a couple of strategic lenses to view organizational design choices. Keep in mind that there is no one "right answer" to Procurement's organizational design choices. The goals of organizational design for Procurement are as follows:

- To build on the earlier assessment of the company's readiness for world-class procurement
- To structure Procurement to meet the company's current and near-term needs
- To prepare Procurement to meet the company's longer-term needs

These choices are fluid and will necessarily evolve as the company changes. Since organizations are dynamic, be prepared to manage changing internal and external expectations.

Note on the use of matrices: A selection of proven matrices is used throughout the design process. They are not intended for mechanistic application; there is no Excel spreadsheet with calculations available to create "the right answer." The matrices are discussion tools to be employed with key stakeholders in order to understand the interplay of the significant criteria. This interplay, as well as the appropriate organizational design, will evolve over time.

Levels of Strategic Impact				
	High			
	Medium			
	Low			
Organizational Impact Assessment Matrix		**Low** (Single site or within a function)	**Medium** (Multiple sites or one region)	**High** (Cross-regions or business units)
		Breadth of Impact		

Historically, the role of the sourcing or category manager encompassed end-to-end responsibility for strategy from creation through implementation. This is now changing to include distinct strategy and implementation roles. We think this is an excellent development and reflects the continued pressure on all employees with implementation responsibilities to address tactical-supply issues. The day-to-day operational pressures of most businesses will supplant strategy-development efforts unless the structure provides clear distinctions in roles and responsibilities.

The following pages depict our recommendations for analyzing and staffing these roles in light of the critical, strategic nature of the underlying categories.

Sourcing and Supplier Management

Principles

- The procurement leader who leads the strategy-development process will be the primary liaison with the suppliers who are selected to fulfill the strategy and, as such, will establish the sourcing strategy for ongoing supplier management (as appropriate for the category segmentation).

- Organizational capability (quantity—amount of capacity and the associated skills or capabilities) must match the inherent organizational complexity and category segmentation.

- Category assessments may change—either category segmentation or the degree to which category goods and services are used across the company.

Sourcing and Supplier-Management Governance Matrix

Category Segmentation	Low (Single site or within a function)	Medium (Multiple sites or across several sites; one region)	High (Cross-regions or businesses)
Strategic	**Keep extremely close – everyone is counting on you** Stakeholder-proximate location	**Keep extremely close – everyone is counting on you** Central/Stakeholder-proximate location	
Preferred	**Stay close and ensure success** Stakeholder-proximate location	**Stay close and ensure success** Stakeholder-proximate location	
Conventional	**Stay connected, and ensure efficiency of efforts.** Location immaterial; excellent stakeholder engagement required regardless of location		
Approved	**Make it work; keep it simple, and mind the cost.** Location immaterial; approximate stakeholder engagement and enabling systems to support compliance management required		

Scope of Enterprise Impact

X-Axis – Scope of Enterprise Impact

- **Low** – Category of spend is narrowly used within a site or function.
- **Medium** – Category of spend is used across a few sites or a region.
- **High** – Category of spend is widely applicable across the company.

Y-Axis – Category Segmentation

As previously applied in the category-review process using the four typical segmentation levels

- Strategic
- Preferred
- Conventional
- Approved

In-depth Commentary by Segmentation Level

Strategic – *Keep extremely close; everyone is counting on you.*

- Business-requirements emphasis – new product development/innovation; outsourced relationships
- Organizational complexity – highly complex and nuanced
- Supplier management focus – complex; innovation/joint teams/outsourced capabilities

Staffing implications – Select only the very best, most capable staff members; provide coaching and mentoring; identify a backup, and develop an "understudy."

Staffing location – Locate the sourcing and supplier management team closest to stakeholders and the procurement leadership team. Direct access to both is a critical success factor. Centralize staffing if the category spans multiple business units or locations.

Preferred – *Stay close, and ensure success.*

- Business-requirements emphasis – process innovation; outsourced relationships; often truly "conventional categories" that are escalated due to current issues
- Organizational complexity – complex and nuanced; may be "under a microscope" if "temporarily escalated in level" due to supply issues
- Supplier-management focus – joint teams for process innovation are established; assurance of supply if the supplier is escalated to a higher level of management intensity as a result of supply issues

Staffing implications – Choose very capable staff with potential for development; basic requirements include problem solving and joint team leadership; excellent developmental role in preparation for leading strategic categories.

Staffing location – Locate the sourcing and supplier management team near the stakeholders and the procurement leadership team. Direct access to both is critical to success. Centralize staffing if the category spans multiple business units or locations.

Conventional – ***Stay connected, and ensure efficiency of efforts.***

- Business-requirements emphasis – basic levels of A/RQSCI; heavy emphasis on cost
- Organizational complexity – less complex due to either the well-established norms of engaging the correct suppliers through defined channels and/or expectations are controlled by accepted policies and practices
- Supplier-management focus – compliance with agreements and support for implementing layered strategy (as applicable); only exception is management

Staffing implications – This is an appropriate proving ground for new staff. It is also an excellent option for distant/telecommuting staffing, either through an internal, shared service/sourcing hub, or outsourced to a third-party category expert. *Note: If outsourced, the sourcing process should be consistent with the internal process and all sourcing; supplier-management-generated materials remain the property of the company (i.e., should remain on the company network or shared cloud domain).*

Staffing location – Locate the sourcing and supplier management team wherever it can be most efficiently placed in terms of cost of staff, space, and other factors. Put all necessary technology in place to facilitate stakeholder and peer interactions (i.e., high-quality video conferencing, personal webcams, etc.)

Approved – ***Make it work; keep it simple, and keep your eye on the cost.***

- Business-requirements emphasis – basic levels of A/RQSCI; heavy emphasis on transaction costs
- Organizational complexity – typically less complex if consumption compliance measures are fully implemented and stakeholder acceptance is high
- Supplier-management focus – compliance with agreements and support for layered-strategy implementation (as applicable); only exception is management

Staffing implications – Most appropriate for remote, lower-cost staffing, either through an internal, shared service/sourcing hub model or outsourced to a third-party category expert. *Note: If the sourcing process is outsourced, it should be consistent with the internal process; all sourcing and supplier-management-generated materials remain the property of the company (i.e., should stay on the company network or shared cloud domain).*

Staffing location – This is the least sensitive group of categories from a location perspective. All necessary technology should be in place to facilitate stakeholder and peer interactions (e.g., high-quality video conferencing, personal webcams, etc.). Use appropriately distributed staff and technologies to address compliance and demand-management strategies.

Recommended Implementation Principles

- Layered strategies will be implemented for all categories regardless of segmentation level.
- Implementation is a complex process of change leadership and project management.
- Implementation of specialized categories may require a professional who is viewed more as a subject-matter expert than as an implementation expert.
- Implementation resources (people, processes, and travel budgets) are functional resources to be shared and prioritized based on aggregate and agreed-upon priorities.

Strategy Implementation Implications

All strategies, whether developed globally, regionally, or locally, will ultimately be implemented at the personal level. This may mean a single functional head for a global indirect category (e.g., HR, Legal, Marketing subspecialty), a small group of key stakeholders, or a globally distributed group of numerous stakeholders. As such, implementation resources and approaches must be tailored to meet the different requirements. Nevertheless, they all share a common theme: Implementation staff should be as close to the stakeholders as possible and perceived as "local."

Strategic – *Keep extremely close; everyone is counting on you.*

- Business-requirements emphasis – new-product development/ innovation; outsourced relationships
- Organizational complexity – highly complex and nuanced

  Staffing implications – dedicated to the respective sourcing leader (i.e., category based)

  Staffing location – close to key stakeholders and, if needed, to key suppliers

Implementation and Change Leadership: In-depth Commentary by Segmentation Levels

Preferred – ***Stay close, and ensure success.***

- Business-requirements emphasis – process innovation; outsourced relationships; often truly "conventional categories" that are escalated due to current issues
- Organizational complexity – complex and nuanced; may be "under a microscope" if the category is "temporarily promoted" due to supply issues

  Staffing implications – shared pool unless purely site- or function-focused AND strategy-implementation requirements are complex; more capable and stakeholder-savvy staffing required

  Staffing location – proximate to key stakeholders and, if necessary, to key suppliers

Conventional – ***Stay connected, and ensure efficiency of efforts.***

- Business-requirements emphasis – basic levels of A/RQSCI; heavy emphasis on cost. *Note: The category can be a "promoted," base category due to higher-order strategy implementation (i.e., outsourcing, etc.).*
- Organizational complexity – less complex, due to either the well-established norms of engaging the correct suppliers through defined channels and/or expectations are controlled by accepted policies and practices

  Staffing implications – shared pool unless purely site- or function-focused AND strategy-implementation requirements are complex

  Staffing location – typically in a pool by region to minimize travel costs and maximize stakeholder familiarity and consistency with accents and languages

Approved – ***Shared Resources***

- Implementation emphasis – basic "strategy steps" focused on consumption patterns and compliance

  Staffing implications – shared-pool resource

  Staffing location – wherever the shared pool is most efficiently located; adequate language capability essential

Summary

Organizational design is a complex topic best addressed with your HR partners. The organizing principles, however, must align with the strategic priorities of the organization and its ability to fund Procurement. The use of distributed and outsourced staff is now commonplace and generally accepted in the appropriate categories and authorized areas of communications, systems support, and program management.

The organization of tomorrow will not be like today's organization. Help prepare your employees to expect change and to see ongoing organizational evolution as the norm.

CPO Insights from Chris

The effectiveness and ultimate success of the procurement organization is governed by the company's needs and its readiness to embrace Procurement's role. Procurement's capabilities must align with the business's priorities. As a leader, in order to position Procurement for success, you must continuously assess the evolution of the company's readiness to embrace Procurement and Procurement's ability to meet the company's changing needs.

Depending on the size and scale of your company, consider the following:

1. As you assess how well you support the business, we recommend that you put strategic categories close to the primary customer and have a relationship model in place in order to be successful in the categories that are not close to the customer.
2. Establish a diverse organization to avoid "groupthink" (term coined by social psychologist Irving Janis in 1972 to describe how groups under considerable pressure often make faulty decisions). Solicit key stakeholder input on the design of the function.
3. Clearly define and address global and regional business needs, now and into the future.
4. As you assess capability, create the right mix of strategic thinkers, process thinkers, and employees who are transactional and execution focused. Be transparent in what you expect of each role. Continuously assess internal capability and benchmark versus outside standards.

TEMPLATE: Procurement Organization Design

Your Name:	Function Area:

Sourcing and Supplier Management Governance Matrix

Category Segmentation			
Strategic	**Keep extremely close – everyone is counting on you** Stakeholder-proximate location		**Keep extremely close – everyone is counting on you** Central / Stakeholder-proximate location
Preferred	**Stay close, and ensure success.** Stakeholder-proximate location		**Stay close, and ensure success.** Stakeholder-proximate location
Conventional	**Stay connected, and ensure efficiency of efforts.** Location immaterial; excellent stakeholder engagement required regardless of location		
Approved	**Make it work, keep it simple, and mind the cost.** Location immaterial; approximate stakeholder engagement and enabling systems to support compliance management required		
	Low (Single site or within a function)	**Medium** (Multiple sites or across several sites; one region)	**High** (Cross-regions or businesses)
	Scope of Enterprise Impact		

X-Axis – Scope of Enterprise Impact:

- High – Category of spend is widely applicable across the company.
- Medium – Category of spend is used across a few sites or a region.
- Low – Category of spend is narrowly used, within a site or function.

Y-Axis – Category Segmentation:

As previously applied in the category-review process using the four typical segmentation levels:

- Strategic
- Preferred
- Conventional
- Approved

Strategic Categories	Stars/High-Potentials	Support Required/Transition Plan
Preferred Categories	**Stars/Learners/High-Potentials**	**Support Required/Transition Plan**
Base/Approved Categories	**Internal Options**	**External Options/Implications**

Step 1 - List the segmented categories/sub-categories down the left-hand side in the applicable areas (strategic, preferred, base and approved).

Step 2 - Assign, if possible, the identified star/high-potential employees to the strategic categories with a first priority and the preferred categories as a second priority.

Step 3 - Identify the transition and support plans required to enable an staff moves between categories (i.e., if the stars/high-potentials were assigned to different categories and must now transition responsibility to somebody else). Note that identified 'learners' are likely to need support in order to succeed with the preferred categories.

Step 4 - Consider the entire range of support options available for base and approved categories including internal staffing and external support/outsourcing and the implications on internal staffing levels and stakeholder change management.

23 Stage Reviews

Topic Area Assessment Statements

Review these statements from your perspective as a procurement leader. If you "strongly agree" with all of the statements, you may wish to skip to the next topic. But, if you have some doubts about any of them, we recommend that you read this chapter and engage in some self-reflection.

- The rigor with which processes are applied is consistent with how important the category is to the company.
- The process application reflects effective and consistent stakeholder engagement.
- The process application reflects how effectively my team and I incorporate strategic insights into category and supplier-management strategies and plans.
- Comprehensive documentation enables seamless transition of responsibility to employees who join the team in the future.
- Individual and department development-and-training plans are linked to the review process.

Topic Introduction: Stage Reviews

Effective strategy development—whether in the form of strategic sourcing or supplier management—takes time. Depending on how complex and critical the category is, this time can range from a couple of weeks to a year. No organization can wait a year to review a strategy and determine whether the strategy is on target and of sufficient quality. Once the time is spent, you can't get it back. Midprocess reviews are the best way to assess how thorough your strategy-development efforts have been.

Stage reviews are visible, tangible demonstrations of Procurement's leadership. They provide an opportunity to coach employees and demonstrate your leadership proficiency in content and process. In short, the stage-review process is a vehicle for you to showcase the breadth and depth of your skills. Thoughtful, empathic leaders, who still expect results, are respected for their range of capabilities. Callous, rude leaders, who focus solely on results and are disrespectful to their people, will be regarded as bullies and probably won't remain in leadership positions for long. Do not underestimate the importance and visibility of these stage-review sessions.

You should set the tone for stage reviews and manage them throughout the process. Do not allow these sessions to become vindictive or punitive. Conversely, don't excuse weak, incomplete performance. It is your job to create a supportive culture of high performance.

As previously mentioned, the underlying sourcing and supplier-management processes include a number of discrete steps—typically, five to seven in each process. The purpose of the stage review is to conduct a comprehensive evaluation after each step.

Topic-Specific Nomenclature

As in most industries, procurement professionals use a range of terminology with specific definitions. The following terms and definitions are used in this section:

- ***None.***

The Tool: Stage Reviews

Stage reviews serve as ongoing internal-quality reviews for the strategic-sourcing and supplier-management processes. These reviews will reveal how well the procurement team understands the processes, as well as highlight key category and supply-market insights. The process of running stage reviews, however, must be carefully designed to ensure that they are effective and efficient. It is too easy for the stage-review process to become cumbersome and time consuming. Finally, use the documentation already present in the strategic-sourcing and supplier-management processes. Do not create redundant presentations solely for the stage reviews. This is a waste of time and does not add any value.

Inputs

- Be sure that all related process documentation corresponds to the appropriate step in the process.
- Many organizations create templates for their sourcing and supplier-management processes. Templates can be helpful but are not necessary for stage reviews to be successful. Don't fall into the trap of thinking that completed templates indicate high-quality work.

Process

For each stage in the process, first ask these questions, and then decide if you agree with the statements that follow:

1. *Does the effort expended by the team on a particular category reflect that category's importance to the company?*
   a) The most important categories require more time because they are inherently more complex than the less-important categories.
   b) The sourcing team applies the appropriate strategic tools.
   c) Global categories must show evidence of global analysis, including variations in underlying stakeholder expectations, business requirements, and supply markets. (It is not enough to reflect the input of the largest markets and ignore the smaller markets).

2. *How are we continuing to engage and inform stakeholders?*
   a) Stakeholder maps are current. The sourcing team tailors communication plans to address key stakeholders' preferences and communication goes far beyond blanket emails.
   b) Communication plans reflect the strategic insights developed throughout the process.
   c) Clear stakeholder input is incorporated into subsequent plans.

3. *Do the resulting strategies and initial implementation plans address the strategic insights revealed in the strategy-development process?*
   a) Capture and address strategic insights that emerge throughout the strategy-development process in the resulting strategy. Effective change management depends on communicating the strategic insights to the stakeholders.

4. *Would the documentation from the stage review enable the next person in this position to seamlessly assume responsibility for the category?*
   a) Team progress documentation is complete (action plans, minutes, decision logs, etc.).
   b) Process documentation (all analysis tools, baseline performance data, market analysis, RFx data, supplier proposals, contracts, etc.) is complete and stored in a way that is consistent with functional-data and information-documentation practices.

   Note: In ALL cases, the documentation presented should be the actual team documentation and not incremental presentations developed solely for the purpose of a stage review.

5. *Is the quality of thought and rigor of application sufficient to continue going forward (i.e., Is the process being used thoughtfully or just a "tick-in-the-box" approach, simply completing another set of templates without thinking about the intent)?*
   a) A RAG analysis of the results is completed and typically means:
      i) Green = approved to continue; no changes required
      ii) Amber = not approved to continue; address the specific (and limited) defects, and return for review of the changes (exception review only)
      iii) Red = not approved; substantial rework required. When all rework is completed, return the entire body of work for review

   Note: We believe that the RAG assessment reflects on both the individual who presents the information AND his/her leader. In too many cases, only the individual is held accountable for the results, which should never occur. True leaders help their people prepare for stage reviews.

6. *Are the results of the stage-review process part of Procurement's broader developmental planning?*
   a) Individual training-and-development plans reflect areas where the individual is strong and can peer-coach others or where the individual is weak and needs peer coaching.
   b) When we observe recurring gaps in performance, we are able to identify the types of training to provide to employees.

Participants

Chair/Reviewers – A member of the procurement leadership team typically chairs the stage reviews. The CPO should chair company-level strategic category reviews, which should include the entire procurement leadership team. Categories at the next level of strategic importance—direct, indirect, capital, and regional—are typically reviewed within the procurement disciplines. The area leader chairs the reviews, which includes all subordinate managers.

Presenter(s) – The sourcing manager, category manager, or supplier manager usually presents his/her work. He/she may include selected team members if specific expertise is required (and allowed by the chair). See observers below. Occasionally, a reviewer (usually, the presenter's manager) will answer questions on behalf of the presenter when questions involve areas that are known only to the reviewer or manager.

Observers – Observers from within the Procurement department and the respective disciplines are typically included. Observers are encouraged to watch and listen but may not interrupt or participate unless they are asked to. On a case-by-case basis, the chair may include other observers from Procurement or from outside of the department. Beware of including too many participants and turning what should be a thoughtful, careful review into a spectacle. Do not allow grandstanding.

Summary

Stage reviews should be expected and part of the normal ways of working. They should result in sufficiently thoughtful and high-quality strategies and plans to ensure successful implementation and change management. Stage reviews are also a test of your technical competence and ability to coach and mentor your staff. Incorporate all of the lessons learned and knowledge gained from the stage reviews into your procurement development plans.

CPO Insights from Chris

Stage reviews must not be seen as merely the process of ticking the box. There are many ways to use the stage-review process so that teams are able to build category strategies that are robust and world class. Comprehensive strategy development helps employees and team members feel confident that they have covered all aspects of the process and prepares them to present to either leadership or their stakeholder communities. Stage reviews can also be a mechanism to identify talented people in the organization and better understand how they think. Stage reviews help identify the potential value across A/RQSCI from all of the included categories and are important in creating a sustained plan for the future. They also enable you to pinpoint areas in which you may need additional resources.

24 Talent Management

Topic Area Assessment Statements

Review these statements from your perspective as a procurement leader. If you "strongly agree" with all of the statements, you may wish to skip to the next topic. But, if you have some doubts about any of them, we recommend that you read this chapter and engage in some self-reflection.

- My team and I identify high-potential employees and provide them with rigorous, thoughtful development.
- My team and I recognize employees who are reluctant to embrace the transformation process and either dismiss them or encourage them to work in other areas of the business.
- The Human Resources function is ready to support the expanded requirements of Procurement's transformation.
- Procurement employees are incented to drive the department's value proposition.

Topic Introduction: Talent Management

Procurement transformation and the ongoing execution of a world-class procurement function require outstanding employees. There are multiple ways to support a world-class procurement function (systems, tools, outsourced capabilities, among others). Nevertheless, the best strategy to deliver world-class procurement capability rests with the employees.

Topic-Specific Nomenclature

As in most industries, procurement professionals use a range of terminology with specific definitions. The following terms and definitions are used in this section:

- ***None.***

The Tool: Talent Management

Every large company uses extensive enterprise resource-management programs, some investing hundreds of millions of dollars in the deployment of SAP and Oracle, with the goal of achieving data for organizational applications. This is a worthy business goal but should not distract from the reality that Procurement is ultimately a people-based team sport. Talent management—identification and development of high performers, management of the core cadre of steady performers, and the removal of poor performers—is a core element of the procurement leader's role. Once the assessment of talent is developed, it will guide your leadership actions and allocation of time. In short, focus on the core group of steady performers and emerging high performers. The low performers will inevitably push for attention (the "squeaky-wheel theory"), and you may be tempted to try to "fix" them. This is almost impossible and will consume all of your management attention. Provide them with the feedback and guidance they need and deserve; then, it is up to them to perform.

The following two-by-two matrix, which is a simple twist on the traditional General Electric/Boston Consulting Group (GE/BCG) Growth-Share Matrix, makes the point quite clearly: Focus on developing stars!

Process	High	**Learner**	**Star**
	Low	**In HR**	**Maverick**
Talent Profiling Matrix		Low	High
		Results	

This simple matrix should be used as a consistent lens to assess all levels within the organization and prioritize support activities.

Y-Axis – Process

- Adoption of the sourcing process
- Adoption of the supplier management process
- Proactive stakeholder engagement
- Actions consistent with the functional ways of working

X-Axis – Results

- Measurable results – typically savings-focused but should include the entire A/RQSCI spectrum

Talent Management: Recommended Approaches

Acquisition

World-class procurement employees know they are valuable. Being aware of the respective supply market is a procurement core competency, and this is never truer than when applied to salaries and benefits. Surveys reflect that high-capability people command excellent packages and salaries. Link your HR support team (particularly the compensation staff) to the marketplace to be sure it is benchmarking current roles with comparable roles in appropriate organizations.

Retention

First and foremost, *retain the stars!* The *stars* deliver excellent results and model processes and functional ways of working. It is real work to develop *stars*, and once they have proven themselves, you need to keep them. There is often a question about what to do with *stars who are eligible for promotion.* You have a choice between two pathways: the "high-professional/individual-contributor" and "management/leadership career." Move only employees who are capable of becoming leaders onto the management/leadership-career ladders. Recognize excellent individual contributors, and confirm their capabilities in appropriate roles. Do not fall into the trap of promoting excellent individual contributors into unsuitable leadership roles. Develop suitable career ladders to recognize and retain their individual talents.

Clearly and objectively identify high-potential employees, and make their development a high priority. High-potential employees are distinguished by the following criteria[1]:

- They know the business.
- Others respect them.
- They are ambitious.
- They work well with others.
- They are willing to take risks.
- They are willing to accept the organization's geographic flexibility requirements.
- They are able to use new tools, processes, and approaches to deliver value.

Avoid selecting *high-potential employees* based solely on the impressions of a single leadership-team member; cross-validate impressions to ensure consistency and avoid rater bias. To confirm alignment between the employee and the potential new role, discuss that individual's personal goals and aspirations with him/her.

1. Adapted from *Profiles International* publication, "Hitting the Mark with High Potentials." http://info.profilesinternational.com/web/website-hitting-the-mark-with-high-potentials/

Second, develop the *learners* who are using the appropriate tools, processes, and ways of working but need support to deliver better results. If they are new to the tools or the broader organizational ways of working, they may be producing subpar results. Hold honest, direct conversations with them about their results, and provide coaching and mentoring to improve their ability to deliver higher-level results.

Third, address the *mavericks* (who produce good results without using the proper processes, tools, or new ways of working) and *in HR* (who don't produce results or use new approaches). The *mavericks* tend to be the most difficult in the organization to address because they deliver big results, know lots of people, and work in ways that are inconsistent with the future of Procurement. (Often, they are focused solely on the lower steps of the strategy staircase negotiations and have little stakeholder engagement.) These are truly hard conversations to engage in, but you must have them. The entire organization is watching to see if the *mavericks* will be required to change their behavior to meet the vision/value proposition of the future.

Those *in HR* who need to be retained are new hires. In order to increase the likelihood of their success, they should be assimilated into procurement processes and assigned to appropriate managers for continuous monitoring and spend categories they understand. Be certain that the staff you work so hard to recruit succeeds once they become part of Procurement!

Exit (Managing Employees out of Procurement)

This cohort of employees largely consists of the unchanging *mavericks* but will also include the incumbent staff members who are incapable of adapting to the new style and culture of the transformed procurement function. This does not mean, however, that they would not become valuable employees in other areas of the company. Separate those who are unwilling to change from those who are incapable of changing, and address them as follows: The "unwilling" should be referred to HR for eventual dismissal; spend no more time on them. The "incapable" should be carefully assessed for their other skills and abilities and referred to appropriate departments or functions for consideration.

Other Issues

Finally, address the broader HR implications of transformation. As mentioned earlier, capable hires demand market pay rates. This frequently leads to escalating offers and potential salary compression/pay-equity issues in the broader workforce. Address these issues proactively with HR. Do not "dare" current employees to test the market; you are likely to lose your *stars* in the process.

Employee compensation and management-by-objectives targets must reflect the entire functional-value proposition. Too often, procurement employees are measured primarily on achievement of savings, which is valuable, but only one element of the A/RQSCI range of business requirements. The entire range—as well as stakeholder, supplier, and functional relationships—must be reflected.

We are increasingly using assessment instruments like the Profiles XT.[2] This instrument, in concert with the full range of HR and developmental-coaching support, provides the individual and his/her manager with key insights into that person's preferences and capabilities. We cannot (yet) recommend them as the primary selection/retention tool but are quite impressed with the comprehensive range of reliable results.

Summary

The Procurement leadership team should regularly review and update the entire talent plan. As you do so, step back and ask yourselves:

- Are you recruiting talent at appropriate and desired levels?
  If not, why not?
- Are you retaining your stars? Your high-potentials? If not, why not?
- Are the stars moving into leadership roles? If not, why not?
- Are you firing or removing the mavericks efficiently? Is HR?
  If not, why not?

How much time are you spending on each of these areas? Those in HR and mavericks will, if you let them, consume all of your time. They should receive the minimum attention possible. Focus your efforts where they will pay immediate and long-term results (i.e., the new hires, learners, high-potentials, and stars).

CPO Insights from Chris

Employee capability is the number one area for a leader to consider. There are many approaches; the ones you choose depend on the culture of the company, as well as on the capability and style of the employees you need. Personality fit is important, and employees' interpersonal skills must fit with the style of the stakeholders. This is vital; a "one-size-fits-all" approach will not work.

The key is to clearly communicate expectations and instruct your leadership team to give feedback to its employees. Procurement's performance bar is raised every year, and employees must keep up with the ever-higher bar. There will be situations in which you have to make hard choices as you go through the process. Our advice: Be fair, but do not hesitate to act.

2. Profiles International instrument is an excellent, comprehensive assessment tool for individuals. We also recommend the 360 tools for current and prospective leaders.

TEMPLATE: Talent Management

<table>
<tr><td colspan="4">Your Name:</td><td>Functional Area:</td></tr>
<tr><td rowspan="2">Process</td><td>High</td><td>Learner</td><td>Star</td><td rowspan="4">Y-Axis – Process
• Adoption of the sourcing process
• Adoption of the supplier-management process
• Pro-active stakeholder engagement
• Actions consistent with the functional ways-of-working
X-Axis – Results
• Measurable results – typically savings-focused but should include the entire A/RQSCI spectrum</td></tr>
<tr><td>Low</td><td>In HR</td><td>Maverick</td></tr>
<tr><td colspan="2" rowspan="2">Talent Profiling Matrix</td><td>Low</td><td>High</td></tr>
<tr><td colspan="2">Results</td></tr>
</table>

<table>
<tr><td rowspan="2">Rank order employees on each parameter</td><td>Process</td><td>Results</td></tr>
<tr><td></td><td></td></tr>
<tr><td rowspan="10">Talent Management Planning</td><td>Stars</td><td>Development Actions</td></tr>
<tr><td></td><td></td></tr>
<tr><td>Learners</td><td>Development Actions</td></tr>
<tr><td></td><td></td></tr>
<tr><td>High-Potentials</td><td>Development Actions</td></tr>
<tr><td></td><td></td></tr>
<tr><td>Mavericks</td><td>Intervention / HR Support Required</td></tr>
<tr><td></td><td></td></tr>
<tr><td>In HR</td><td>Intervention / HR Support Required</td></tr>
<tr><td></td><td></td></tr>
</table>

About the Authors

Erik Stavrand is a founding partner at Catchlight Consulting, LLC, which is dedicated to helping clients achieve commercial excellence through strategic procurement and change management. An expert executive coach, Erik works with procurement and sales executives in global blue-chip companies across a wide range of industries. With experience in hands-on management in the pharmaceutical and life-sciences fields, Erik is a skilled and confident instructor and coach. Currently, he is managing consultant for a global medical firm where he is responsible for all education of internal staff, reorganization of the function, and coaching procurement leaders. Erik is a Certified Professional in Supply Management (CPSM), a Senior Professional in Human Resources (SHRM), a Professional Certified Coach (PCC), and a qualified Myers-Briggs Type Indicator (MBTI) practitioner. Erik's previous certifications included Certified Benefits Professional (CBP) and Certified Quality Engineer (CQE).

Chris Shanahan is vice president Global Procurement for Becton, Dickinson and Company (BD), a leading international medical technology company that manufactures medical devices, instrument systems, and reagents. In his current role as a senior procurement and supply-chain executive, Chris possesses a special aptitude for leading complex teams and building trust across international boundaries. He heads up a diverse team of more than three hundred people in over twenty locations around the world, manages over $6 billion in spend, and sits on BD's leadership team and integrated supply-chain operating committees. Chris joined BD in Ireland in 2000 and moved to the United States in 2005 to lead Global Procurement Worldwide along with Global Real Estate, Construction, Corporate Aviation and Facility Operations. Chris sits on the advisory board for the Supply Chain Program at Farleigh Dickinson University and sits on the executive advisory council for the Hackett Group.

74897539R00142

Made in the USA
Columbia, SC
15 September 2019